LOST GOLD
OF THE DARK AGES

---❖---

War, Treasure, and the
Mystery of the Saxons

CAROLINE
ALEXANDER

Principal Photography by Robert Clark

NATIONAL GEOGRAPHIC

WASHINGTON, D.C.

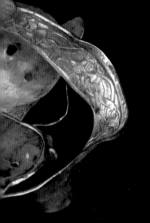

RON HASKINS, 1964-2011
WHO EXCELLED IN EVERY ART AND ARTIFICE OF WAR.

CONTENTS

OPPOSITE: Harking back to Saxon times, the outline of a sword is carved into a stone slab at Jarrow Monastery.
PAGE 1: A finely decorated piece from the hoard.
PAGES 2-3: Some 3,500 finely wrought fragments of gold and silver, composed mostly of war gear, were found with the Staffordshire Hoard.
PAGES 4-5: Despite a series of imposing fortifications and defenses, such as Hadrian's Wall, the Roman army left Britain in the fifth century, opening the region to Anglo-Saxon advances from the east.
PAGES 6-7: Marsh grass on the Northumbrian shore near Bamburgh, which may have been the seat of power for native Britons until A.D. 547, when it was captured by the Anglo-Saxon Ida of Bernicia

INTRODUCTION

Terry Herbert parked his car on a side road and, carrying his metal detector, opened the gate and went into the field. This was his second visit. He had spent four hours here a week earlier but had found nothing, just modern junk. Climbing a low ridge running across the field, he walked to an area that he hadn't searched before and turned on his metal detector. Swinging the detector, he walked up and down for 15 minutes before the machine gave a bleep; there was something there. He dug in to the soft, floury soil and picked up his find. It looked like a piece of brass, thin and twisted, with a pin sticking out of one side. As the metal glittered in the sunlight for the first time in 1,400 years, he realized that it was gold. Scarcely able to contain his excitement, Terry worked on; he found another piece, then another; slowly he moved toward the center of the hoard, his metal detector now buzzing continuously. Sometimes he would dig after a signal and three or four objects would fall out on the soil. Even when he put the detector down, it lay there buzzing.

At about 3 p.m. Terry went down to see Fred Johnson, the farmer. Fred had been born on the farm and had lived there all of his life. Terry showed him the twisted gold sword fittings, pommels, and garnet-set strips, still covered in earth. Fred was skeptical, and only later did he come to realize the items' importance. His countryman's sound good sense has never left him; when I claimed that this was the best crop that had ever come off the field, he corrected me: The food the field had produced was more important—you can't eat gold.

OPPOSITE: Many of the pieces in the hoard are damaged, but this looks more like simple breaking and folding rather than systematic destruction.

LOST GOLD OF THE DARK AGES

One of the biggest mysteries presented by the Staffordshire Hoard is this strip of bent gold, which bears a warlike inscription from the Latin Bible. It reads, "Rise up O Lord, and may Thy enemies be scattered and those who hate Thee flee from Thy face." The lettering most likely dates from the seventh century, and the strip is believed to have originally been part of a cross.

Terry worked until 5 p.m. before deciding that enough was enough. He had found 50 or 60 objects, 12 or 15 pommel caps, two gold and garnet pyramids, and a bar of metal bearing strange lettering and a gold cross, folded around the jewels that once had decorated it. While digging this, Terry had seen something sticking out of the ground: a golden snake.

On returning the following day, Terry found that it had been raining. He started searching and, within minutes, was again finding item after item, sometimes in holes that he had already dug. This was getting desperate. The most striking find of the second day was a gold mount decorated with two birds of prey holding a fish in their talons. He also picked up a second, smaller cross; one of its arms was missing, but it turned up about eight yards away. It rained on and off for the next two days, and Terry kept dodging the thunderstorms that swept over the hill. It was very dramatic; the elements seemed to be marking the hoard's return to the world of man. Terry was acutely aware of a real threat: The site lay in the angle of two busy main roads, one being Watling Street, the old Roman road. Would anyone passing see him and wonder why he was spending days on this spot? Among metal detectors there was, unfortunately, a criminal element that

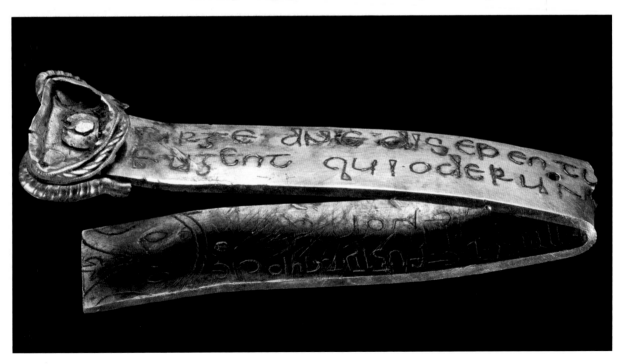

would see this site as suitable for nefarious attentions. Terry hated leaving the site each evening and was relieved when he returned each day to find all was well.

By the fifth day the number of finds had fallen off, but there were still surprises. One of the most memorable objects—a silver-gilt helmet cheekpiece with processions of weird animals—was found on day five. In an area about six feet square Terry picked up 21 lumps of clay with metal fragments sticking out of them. He wisely decided to leave them alone and bagged them for further treatment. He was beginning to see a pattern in the finds: There was one main area with a second concentration two to three yards to the south. From these the plow had scattered the objects down the field for about 40 yards. Terry was now very tired and was not sleeping well. It was time to call in the archaeologists.

Duncan Slarke, Finds Liaison Officer for Staffordshire, was at his desk in Birmingham Museum when he received a phone call from John Hayden, Terry Herbert's cousin. Duncan sat, amazed, as John related what had been found; it sounded incredible. That evening Duncan went to see Terry at home. On the table stood a plastic box, which was opened to reveal the stuff of dreams. Duncan's first comment was "Wow!" He went through the contents of the box and said, "Unbelievable, magical . . . one of these finds would have been important, but this lot: WOW!" Terry then dropped the bombshell: "There's another four boxes," he said. Working late that night, Duncan made notes. Eventually he left with the boxes. Responsibility for the hoard had moved on.

Duncan contacted the organizations that needed to be involved, and there was a meeting of most of them during the following week at the museum in Birmingham. There were representatives from Birmingham Museum and Art Gallery and English Heritage—the body responsible for archaeology in England—and archaeologists from Staffordshire County Council. The Portable Antiquities Scheme was represented by me, Duncan, and Dr. Roger Bland, head of the department of Portable Antiquities and Treasure at the British Museum. We were awestruck by the beauty of what had been found, excited by its historical importance, yet scared stiff that it was our responsibility. Fortunately, fright can do wonderful things, and everyone rose to the occasion. It was clear that work had to be done on the find spot; Terry hadn't found everything. Bill Klemperer from English Heritage said, "Just get some archaeologists out there and sort it out." Then there was the legal side: There would need to be a coroner's inquest on the hoard, but he would need a report on what was found.

Roger Bland, who is responsible for treasure, asked me if I could do a catalog, and so, over the next eight weeks, the hoard was cataloged. Security was still an issue, and a

Archaeologists at the British Museum, including Kevin Leahy, National Finds Adviser for the Portable Antiquities Scheme (middle), study the objects from the Staffordshire Hoard, saved from the soil in what was once the Kingdom of Mercia.

24-hour guard was set up on the site. There was a complete news blackout; until the day of the inquest and press launch, no one outside the group knew of the discovery.

The excavation was carried out by a small team from Birmingham University led by Bob Burrows. They worked for four very wet weeks and, assisted by Terry Herbert, recovered and plotted the positions of everything they found. Terry felt his hoard moving away: "The burden was lifting; they still needed me and my metal detector, but I was slowly losing my hoard. It's hard to describe what I felt; I knew I could never keep it, but being taken away as more people became involved, I was losing it."

Fred Johnson often visited the site to see what was being found. Looking at the finds, he "could understand how the archaeologists got as excited as they did; the workmanship is incredible." He was also impressed by the archaeologists themselves, struggling in the wet, and said they were "incredible people."

We never found the thing that we most wanted: a context for the hoard, something to help date it or tell us why it had been buried. A pit or a pot from which it came, the remains of an associated building, anything that might provide a context. There was nothing; every bit of the hoard came from the plow soil. As they carried out geophysical surveys, scientists looked for electrical or magnetic anomalies that might reveal something beneath the ground, but there was nothing relating to the hoard.

Out of the rain, and helped by my wife, Dianne, I worked on the catalog of finds for the inquest. It was an unforgettable experience. Bag after bag was opened, and each object and fragment was weighed, measured, and recorded on a computer. We were the first people to be able to really look at the find; we saw strange, interlaced animals, their jaws locked around each other. As we worked we knew that we were in the presence of greatness. It was humbling.

KEVIN LEAHY
JULY 2011

Notes on the Treasure

Searching for archaeological finds with a metal detector is legal in England as long as the landowner agrees and the site is not on the list of Ancient Monuments. When metal detectors became popular in the 1970s, many archaeologists were concerned that people were removing objects from sites and destroying important evidence. On the thin upland soils this concern was justified, but the situation was different in the heavily cultivated counties of eastern England (Norfolk, Suffolk, and Lincolnshire). Here, the intensification of agriculture since World War II had led to a massive destruction of sites, and, by recording objects picked up by the detector operators, we could at least salvage something from the wreck. Criminals have used metal detectors to loot sites, and even excavations, but overall the instruments have led to an increase in our knowledge. Metal objects left in the plowed soil do not survive and, unless they are recovered, we will know nothing about them or the sites.

THE PORTABLE ANTIQUITIES SCHEME

The Portable Antiquities Scheme is a national project set up in 1997 to record archaeological finds made by metal-detector users and other members of the public. The program is based at the British Museum but has 40 local liaison officers covering the whole of England and Wales and six National Advisors (I am one of them) who ensure standards. This web-based program has now recorded more than 700,000 finds, all of which can be seen by visiting www.finds.org.uk. There is nothing like this organization anywhere else in the world, and it has led to massive expansion of our knowledge.

TREASURE TROVE AND TREASURE

"Treasure" is one of the peculiarities of the English legal system but, until it was reformed in 1996, it was even more peculiar. Basically, all finds of gold and silver, hoards of coins, and prehistoric metalwork belong to the Crown. To be treasure, a find must be more than 300 years old and contain more than 10 percent gold or silver. Single coins are not considered to be treasure, but any hoard of more than ten base-metal coins may be treasure. Hoards of prehistoric bronze may also be treasure.

The decision of whether or not a find is treasure is made by the district coroner, representing the Crown (the Queen and her government). If it is treasure, it will be offered to museums in the area or, in some cases, the British Museum. If the museums are not interested an object will be disclaimed and returned to the finder, but if they want to acquire it, the find will go before the Treasure Valuation Committee. The TVC takes advice from antiquity dealers who estimate how much a find would sell for at auction. Once a valuation is accepted by the finder, landowner, and interested museum, the museum has to raise the money to buy it from the Crown, which then makes an award of the full market value; this award is shared by the finder and the landowner. The payment of rewards has successfully motivated people to report their finds and has resulted in expanded museum collections throughout the country. There are also penalties for failures to report treasure. Archaeologists who find treasure during the course of their work are not entitled to any reward.

The old law of treasure trove was an odd phenomenon from medieval times. Something would only be considered treasure trove if it was buried with the intention of recovering it. This was not too difficult with a pot of coins—someone's piggy bank was clearly intended to be retrieved—but it was more difficult with something like the Sutton Hoo ship burial. No one intended going back for that (well, not legally, anyway), and that magnificent discovery was not treasure trove. It was returned to the landowner, who generously gave it to the nation. Goodness knows what the old law would have made of the Staffordshire find; we have no clue whether or not anyone ever intended to dig it up.

PRELUDE

News of the hoard's discovery electrified not only the general public, but also the wide community of Anglo-Saxon scholars and specialists. No one had seen anything like it. Previously, there had been discoveries of hoards of coins and other precious objects dating from the long Roman occupation of Britain, as well as discoveries of spectacular Anglo-Saxon burial sites. But the objects pulled from the earth of a Staffordshire field in July 2009 were something novel—a hoard of gold, silver, and objects set with garnets from early Anglo-Saxon times. The quality of the workmanship that had woven the intricate animal-motif cloisonné and had laid the dainty filigree was of the highest order, leading some to remark that the hoard was the metalwork equivalent of such legendary illuminated manuscripts as the Lindisfarne Gospels or the Book of Kells.

Consisting of some 3,500 pieces from hundreds of individual objects that filled 244 bags, the Staffordshire Hoard was remarkable not only for what was in it, but also for what was not. There were no domestic or feminine objects; almost everything that could be identified was military in character. There were sword pommel fittings and saddle pieces, scabbard mounts and strap buckles, hilt ornaments and helmet fittings—but no women's brooches or other jewelry. Also remarkable was that many objects bore evidence of deliberate mutilation, of having been wrenched apart and bent and folded with determined effort. The hoard, then, was a pile of expensive, broken military hardware deposited for unknown reasons 1,300 years ago in a politically and militarily turbulent region in turbulent times.

Who buried the hoard? And why? Thrilling and historic, the Staffordshire Hoard was, above all, enigmatic. And in order to attempt to understand the circumstances of the hoard's burial it is necessary to draw upon the rich and diverse material that historians and archaeologists working in this era have amassed. Changing approaches to archaeology, as well as new technologies developed over recent years, make this a particularly exciting time for Anglo-Saxon studies.

The Staffordshire Hoard, then, is our guiding talisman through the murky, rugged, and fascinating world of the Anglo-Saxons. It will lead us on a journey that traverses the ruined landscape of Rome's occupation of Britain and the settlements of the earliest Anglo-Saxon immigrants. It will take us through misty lore, brushing against King Arthur and skirting dragons, as well as to such revelatory technologies as DNA samplings and stable-isotope analysis, to warrior graves and sword rituals, to *Beowulf* and the magnificent English language. This journey is our best way of understanding why, in approximately A.D. 650, some unknown agent chose to bury a multimillion-dollar hoard of gold in the Staffordshire ground.

CHAPTER ONE

THE COMING
OF THE SAXONS

"For the fire of vengeance...spread from sea to sea...and did not cease, until destroying the neighboring towns and lands, it reached the other side of the island, and dipped its red and savage tongue in the western ocean."

— GILDAS

THE COMING OF THE SAXONS

For the fire of vengeance . . . spread from sea to sea," wrote the monk Gildas, in the mid-sixth century A.D., of the arrival of the Angle and Saxon tribes to Britain from northern Europe. His treatise, *On the Ruin of Britain,* is the primary account we have of the murky period that saw the coming of what he terms "the fierce and impious Saxons": ". . . and did not cease, until, destroying the neighboring towns and lands, it reached the other side of the island, and dipped its red and savage tongue in the western ocean."

Written not so much to record history as to rebuke and chastise Britons for their evil ways, the treatise is a sermon, and it serves Gildas's purpose to exaggerate the sufferings inflicted on the island as a just retribution from God. Today historians challenge his claim that the entirety of Britain was vanquished by Anglo-Saxon invaders who put the island to the torch and sword. At the same time, the period of the settlement of Britain by Germanic tribes in the fifth and sixth centuries was indeed tumultuous. To understand this tumult in its proper context, it is necessary to pull back further and to survey Britain as it was before Angles or Saxons or Jutes or Frisians or any other northern European tribes had designs upon its shores—in other words, to scan briefly the three and a half centuries during which Britain had been Britannia, a province of Imperial Rome; for the fate of Rome is integral to the movements of the Saxons.

According to the historian Cassius Dio, the troops mustered at Boulogne across the English Channel in the spring of A.D. 43 for what was to be Rome's first successful

OPPOSITE: Roman general and statesman Gaius Julius Caesar crosses the English Channel from western France to southern England, 54 B.C.

PREVIOUS PAGES: Hadrian's Wall once formed the 73-mile northernmost frontier of the Roman Empire. Its remains, visible atop the craggy bluff, are now a popular hiking trail in northern England.

The Roman emperor Claudius, conqueror of Britain, is depicted by this life-size bronze statue.

invasion of Britain had at first balked, "indignant at the prospect of campaigning outside the known world"—an eloquent indication of how remote the island lay from continental civilization. This ultimately successful campaign of 43, under Emperor Claudius, vindicated two inconclusive attempts that had been made almost a century earlier by the great Julius Caesar. Caesar had been checked by the guerrilla tactics of the British, by their skilled use of horses and chariots and tendency to vanish into the woods, and most of all by a sudden, devastating storm that had destroyed much of his anchored fleet. His failure notwithstanding, Caesar left a valuable description of the island and its inhabitants as seen through Roman eyes:

The interior portion of Britain is inhabited by those of whom they say that it is handed down by tradition that they were born in the island itself: the maritime portion by those who had passed over from the country of the Belgae [northern Gaul, or modern France] for the purpose of plunder and making war ... The number of the people is countless, and their buildings exceedingly numerous ... The most civilized of all these nations are they who inhabit Kent, which is entirely a maritime district, nor do they differ much from the Gallic customs. Most of the island inhabitants do not sow corn, but live on milk and flesh, and are clad with skins. All the Britons, indeed, dye themselves with woad, which occasions a bluish color, and thereby have a more terrible appearance in fight. They wear their hair long, and have every part of their body shaved except their head and upper lip."

What the Romans wanted from Britain is unclear. It was later rumored that Caesar "was led to invade Britannia by the hope of getting pearls, and that in comparing their size he sometimes weighed them with his own hand." In his own memoirs, however, Caesar spoke lightly of Britain's assets, remarking that "tin is produced in the midland regions; in the maritime, iron; but the quantity of it is small"—meager commodities that would not seem to have justified the expense and effort of an 800-ship, 27,000-man invasion. He had also noted, however, that "in almost all the wars with the Gauls assistance had been furnished to our enemy from that country," meaning Britain; Caesar's expressed objectives, then, seem to have been mostly tactical. It was also true, however, that Britain had traded with continental Europe and the Mediterranean centuries before the coming of the Romans, and in later times, when the island was better known, it was well regarded, according to the first-century geographer Strabo, for exports of "corn, cattle, gold, silver, and iron . . . and also skins, and slaves, and dogs sagacious in hunting." (Eventually, in the course of Roman rule, Britannia would also be known for its hooded woolen coats and beer.) Possibly the first attempt was among other things a matter of prestige, and the failed invasions only sharpened later imperial resolve.

By A.D. 47, southern England was under Roman rule, and Britain as a whole had been claimed for the empire. Like other imperial provinces, Britannia became subject to taxation, Roman law (although the native population still used local laws), and use of Latin as a lingua franca—all the usual baggage of a colonial occupation. With Roman efficiency, a network of roads and other infrastructure for the movement of troops, trade, and communication was established. Despite Caesar's observation that the number of Britain's people "is countless, and their buildings exceedingly numerous," the archaeological record indicates that prior to the Romans, Britain had no settlements large enough to be called towns; in contrast, archaeologists have found some hundred walled towns or small settlements dating from the Roman occupation, along with evidence of countless Roman-era villages. London itself—Londinium— was developed from a trading center on the Thames. In the larger towns public services such as the supply of water and sewage disposal were superior to anything available in later medieval times.

While Roman development projects created previously nonexistent urban landscapes, the majority of the new province's estimated 1.5 to 3 million inhabitants lived rural lives, which, far as they were from administrative centers, seem to have continued more or less as before. The effects of Roman conquest appeared in the countryside; rural settlements suddenly had access to trinket jewelry, imported pottery, and even glass. Buildings in Roman style, villas, were built. The villas, many of which were working farms, adopted amenities particularly suited to Britain, such as central heating and heated floors—innovations appreciated by a people whose "sky is obscured by continual rain and cloud," as the Roman historian Tacitus, writing at the end of the first century A.D., famously observed.

Popular Roman institutions, such as public baths and, in some towns, theaters and temples, helped spread Roman culture

A first-century Roman tomb now in Hexham Abbey contains this memorial to a standard bearer, a coveted position in the Roman army.

among the economic and political elite, as did the sheer attraction and novelty of all things Roman. Tacitus, citing a strategy of the Roman general Agricola (who was his father-in-law) on campaign in Britain, gives a vivid and cynical account of how a conquered people can be led to abandon their own long-held customs for new fashions:

> *He likewise provided a liberal education for the sons of the chiefs, and showed such a preference for the natural powers of the Britons over the industry of the Gauls that they who lately disdained the tongue of Rome now coveted its eloquence. Hence, too, a liking*

> *sprang up for our style of dress, and the "toga" became fashionable. Step by step they were led to things that dispose to vice, the lounge, the bath, the elegant banquet. All this in their ignorance, they called civilization, when it was but a part of their servitude.*

BRITAIN BEFORE THE ROMANS

When the legions of Julius Caesar and later Emperor Claudius fought to control the Isle of Britain, who were they fighting? The Romans dubbed the natives Britons, but we don't know what they called themselves. It's likely there was no single name, as there was no single nation—but their material culture indicates they were Celts, who, linked by languages, originally came from central and northwestern Europe and mixed with still earlier inhabitants of the islands. From about 700 B.C., as the Celts moved across the British Isles, they established small chiefdoms and engaged in constant warfare. Massive hill forts attested to the unsettled nature of the society.

Well before the "civilizing" arrival of the Romans, Britons had already mastered fine metal arts and international trade, and they lived in a flourishing agriculture-based civilization (despite Caesar's description of them as living exclusively "on flesh and milk"). Their houses were earthen and wood, but graves of this period are generally rare, so very few material remains have come down to us. The few we have may be due to their religion: They created beautifully wrought shields and swords, examples of which have been found ritually deposited with other objects in rivers or bogs—perhaps offerings to earth gods.

Their worship was nature based, with a veneration of the oak tree as a protective force, and their ceremonies appear to have taken place outdoors. Caesar and other early writers described a priest class called druids, though there is little physical evidence they existed.

The main impact of the Roman conquest was in Britain's south and east, where towns and villas developed. North and west, in the so-called military zone, the impact of Rome was much smaller, and Britons continued their traditional lifestyles, though with some exposure to Roman culture. The separation from the continental Celts allowed a distinctly British Celtic culture to evolve. Though never held by Rome, Ireland remarkably adopted Roman Christianity and became a beacon of learning during the Dark Ages. ■

This rare bronze head was discovered in a pre-Roman cremation burial in Hertfordshire.

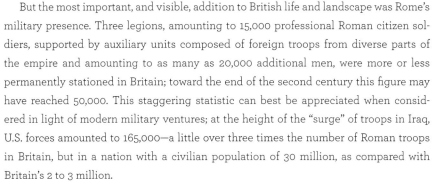

Inlaid with silver and black niello, this first-century bronze statuette depicts Nero as Alexander the Great.

But the most important, and visible, addition to British life and landscape was Rome's military presence. Three legions, amounting to 15,000 professional Roman citizen soldiers, supported by auxiliary units composed of foreign troops from diverse parts of the empire and amounting to as many as 20,000 additional men, were more or less permanently stationed in Britain; toward the end of the second century this figure may have reached 50,000. This staggering statistic can best be appreciated when considered in light of modern military ventures; at the height of the "surge" of troops in Iraq, U.S. forces amounted to 165,000—a little over three times the number of Roman troops in Britain, but in a nation with a civilian population of 30 million, as compared with Britain's 2 to 3 million.

The Roman troops dispersed among the many garrisons and forts in the north and west must have been, with their constant military exercises and training maneuvers and dashing games of display, a conspicuous, daunting, and possibly even glamorous presence. More practically, garrisons and forts of salaried soldiers far from home were a valuable source of income for merchants of the nearby settlements. These active garrisons do not take into account the thousands of *veterani,* ex-soldiers pensioned off in land grants in cities like Colchester and Lincoln.

Why were there so many troops in Britain? Some would like to credit their necessity to the unquenchable fighting spirit of the colonized native Britons, balking at the Roman yoke. A less romantic explanation is that Britain's location, at "the end of the world," and an island at that, made it a convenient holding center for crack troops who could only with difficulty meddle in the politics of the empire. The first Roman troops to make a successful invasion, we recall, had been reluctant "of campaigning outside the known world." If a Roman army was reluctant to venture into the stormy North Atlantic, how unlikely it must have seemed that any other foreign forces would. The likely foes were well known and close to home: the Picts, the tattooed (in Latin *pictus*) tribes who inhabited what was to become Scotland and who, being proficient sailors, raided the eastern coastland as well as the northern borderland; and the Scotti, tribes from Ireland and also sea raiders. As troublesome as these tribes were over the years, their efforts never amounted to much more than periodic harassment that was always quelled by a single, professional Roman campaign.

Rome's troubles in Britain grew apace with its broader troubles on the Continent. Germanic tribes had been moving westward from the mid- to late third century, their progress intermittently checked by a series of campaigns, and scholars estimate that the Saxons began to make raids on Britain around

Roman Britannia
circa A.D. 150

ANTONINE WALL

Dere Street

Mare Germanicum
(North Sea)

HADRIAN'S WALL
Arbeia (South Shields)
Coria
(Corbridge)
Luguvalium
(Carlisle)

Cataractonium
(Catterick)

Isle of Man

Isurium Brigantum
(Aldborough)
Eboracum
(York)

Mare Hibernicum
(Irish Sea)

Mamucium
(Manchester)
Lindum
(Lincoln)

Trent

Ermine Street

HIBERNIA
(IRELAND)

Segontium
(Caernarfon)
Deva
(Chester)

Venta
Icenorum
(Caistor St.
Edmund)

Viroconium
(Wroxeter)
Letocetum
Ratae
(Leicester)
Durobrivae
(Water-Newton)

Staffordshire
Hoard

Durovigutum
(Godmanchester)

Venonae
(High Cross)

CAMBRIA
(WALES)

Watling Street

Fosse Way

Moridunum
(Carmarthen)
Glevum
(Gloucester)
Camulodunum
(Colchester)

Akeman Street

Verulamium
(St. Albans)

Isca
(Caerleon)
Corinium
(Cirencester)

Tamesis   Thames

Londinium
(London)

Durovernum
(Canterbury)

Portway

Calleva Atrebatum
(Silchester)

Sorviodunum
(Salisbury)
Venta
Belgarum
(Winchester)

Stane Street

Dubris
(Dover)

Lindinis
(Ilchester)

Clausentum
(Southampton)

Noviomagus
Reginorum
(Chichester)

Isca
Dumnoniorum
(Exeter)
Durnovaria
(Dorchester)

Mare Britannicum
(English Channel)

— Roman road

0   50 miles

0   50 kilometers

Built in the 12th century by Henry I, Portchester Castle utilizes the defenses of a Roman fort at the head of Portsmouth Harbor.

FOLLOWING PAGES: Though it was likely under construction when Hadrian visited Britain in 122, Hadrian's Wall was the most fortified border in the Roman Empire. Recent scholarship suggests the wall may have served control and customs purposes.

the same time. When exactly Rome began to lose its grip on the island province, however, is impossible to establish, the archaeological record being mixed and the written sources meager. Fortifications suggest one story: Between approximately A.D. 270 and 330, a string of massive fortresses was built on Britain's eastern and southern coastline, implying preparations against new invaders. Similarly, the British line of defense was mirrored across the channel in northern France. Recently, some historians have argued that these "defenses" were actually giant storehouses, not garrisons—signs of Britain's prosperity and stable social infrastructure, rather than of decline. Yet the location of the forts, solidly facing the sea, and their general lack of connection to road networks that would be necessary for transport tend to support the traditional view that the forts were outward looking and defensive: Britain's island status had always been perceived as protective, but this complacency had been based on the assumption that potential foes would not be seafarers. The fortified shore is referred to by name in a rare Roman document,

LOST GOLD OF THE DARK AGES

HADRIAN'S WALL

In an attempt to consolidate the empire and end troubles from Barbarians in Britain's north, the Roman emperor Hadrian built a 15-foot-high wall along the northern border. Ten feet thick, it ran for 73 miles, traversing Britain from Carlisle on the west coast to Newcastle on the east. Seven thousand men guarded its ramparts.

With the wall's many gates, the guards could also now control ingress and egress, tax customs and goods, and prevent smuggling.

Recognizing that a good army is a happy army, the Romans built elaborate forts every five miles along the wall. Each fort could house between 500 and 1,000 troops.

Local people quickly adapted to the wall. Since Roman armies traditionally fed and clothed themselves locally, communities began to evolve around the forts. Thus, a military barricade soon became a community, a culture, and then a thriving and prosperous area.

All that changed, however, when Emperor Hadrian died of heart and liver failure in July 138. Hadrian's successor, Antoninus Pius, pushed the frontier farther north with the construction of turf-and-timber defenses across Britain. This line was not held for long, however, and soon the army withdrew to Hadrian's Wall and manned it until the Romans' final departure.

When the Britons chose Constantine III, one of three homegrown British emperors, as their own emperor in A.D. 407, they cut themselves off from the rest of the Roman Empire. When money stopped coming in from Rome, the soldiers who had at one time garrisoned the wall were withdrawn. Some turned to farming, joined independent armies, or left for other countries. Hadrian's Wall had effectively become a mere landmark on the English landscape. ■

Hadrian, depicted on a bronze statue found in the Thames River near London Bridge in 1834

Bacchus, the Roman god of wine, rides a tiger in this restored mosaic from the first or second century found at Leadenhall Street, London, in 1803.

the *Notitia Dignitatum,* or "List of High Offices," dating from around A.D. 395. A curt inventory of military resources that includes fortifications, the list cites a *comes litoris Saxonici,* or a "count" or military officer "of the Saxon shore"—a suggestive name. Similarly, established forts on the western coast, in what is now modern Wales, were kept manned and reinforced, as were sites along the northwest and northeast coasts, some with signal stations attached to cavalry posts. Thus, to the north, east, south, and west Britain was ringed with stout defenses bespeaking a state of high alert.

And there is written evidence of trouble. "During this period practically the whole Roman world heard the trumpet-call of war, as savage peoples stirred themselves and raided the frontiers nearest to them," wrote Ammianus Marcellinus, a historian and former soldier writing close to the events in the fourth century A.D.: "The Picts, Saxons, Scots and Attacotti were bringing continual misery upon Britain . . . a concerted attack by the barbarians had reduced the province of Britain to the verge of ruin." The so-called *barbarica conspiratio,* or barbarian conspiracy, of A.D. 367 to 368, whether a true conspiracy or a coincidental series of independent raids, was disruptive enough to require a lengthy campaign to restore Roman rule and order: Ominously, Pictish raiders from Scotland had been aided by a revolt of Roman scouts to the north of Hadrian's Wall, Britain's northern frontier.

Ironically, this same fourth century—riven, it would seem, with chronic border anxiety and unrest as well as turmoil in the restless army—has also been called a Golden Age. This is the time when country villas were built and expanded—600 have been identified in Britain. An increasing use of mosaic floors—a conspicuous luxury—appears at this time. The term Golden Age is overblown, but the evidence suggests that the elite and landed gentry, at least, enjoyed notable prosperity—the benefit of a wide social discrepancy between the rich and poor; and this expansion of villas could be a manifestation

LOST GOLD OF THE DARK AGES

of the flight of the aristocracy from declining towns. A number of remarkable treasure hoards dating from this time have also been found. On the one hand, the high quality and value of these objects indicates the level of disposable wealth enjoyed by the prosperous; on the other hand, the manner of disposal—hidden in the ground—is suggestive of unsettled times. The Mildenhall Treasure, a spectacular, highly decorated silver dinner service; the Thetford Hoard and silver vessels with Christian symbols from Water Newton; the Corbridge Lanx—these fourth-century Roman finds are by no means the earliest hoards in Britain, nor the last, but are an impressive slice of a remarkable tradition.

Undoubtedly, rumors of this kind of wealth kept the barbarian raiders coming; treasure and slaves, the objects of their raids, were there for the snatching. A poignant testimony of a slave raid is given by St. Patrick, who recalls in his *Confession* how his father "had a small villa nearby where I was taken captive. I was at that time about sixteen years of age . . . I was taken into captivity in Ireland with many thousands of people."

The erratic miscellany of sources that is the sparse historical record for this critical period now provides equally erratic glimpses of Britain's lurching decline, mirroring the turmoil on the Continent that increasingly held Rome's attention. In 402, one of the two British field armies was recalled to help in the defense of Rome against the Visigoths, and there is evidence that from this year onward the British garrisons were unpaid. In 406, the army revolted, putting forward a succession of weak pretenders to the throne. The same year, the last of these military emperors, Constantine III—"a worthless soldier of the lowest rank," according to the Venerable Bede, writing from older records in A.D. 731—left Britain to quell rebellions in Gaul and took with him the last remaining elements of the field army, although miscellaneous other troops may have remained. After this date, the archaeological record shows that the importation of coinage—money—from the Roman mints ceased, an unambiguous indicator of economic decline. According to the *Gallic Chronicle* (a document written some four decades after the events it describes), the following year, A.D. 408, saw "the province of Britain laid waste by Saxons; in Gaul the barbarians prevailed and Roman power diminished." A new and valuable voice comes from the Greek historian Zosimus, who, writing in the early sixth century, reports,

An engraved Roman carnelian jewel from the fourth century depicts Venus and Cupid protected by the armor of Mars.

When discovered in Scotland in 1919, this hoard of Roman silver tableware and other items, weighing more than 53 pounds, had been crushed or cut up for division.

"[T]he barbarians above the Rhine, assaulting without hindrance, reduced the inhabitants of the Brettanic island and some of the Celtic peoples to defecting from the Roman rule and living their own lives, independent from the Roman laws. The Britons therefore took up arms and, braving the danger on their own behalf, freed their cities from the barbarian threat."

In the vacuum left by Rome, it appears that military and political authority was grasped by local chiefs, or "tyrants," as one source calls them. Two years later, also according to Zosimus, petitioners in Britain sent a letter to Emperor Honorius begging assistance—apparently, despite their revolt and the loss of the legions, the British

still regarded themselves as subjects of Rome. But Rome was now beyond giving aid: According to Bede's stark summary, "[A]fter this the Romans ceased to rule in Britain, almost 470 years after Gaius Julius Caesar had come to the island." In other words, in A.D. 410, Rome had cut herself free of all responsibility for Britain's defense, and the island was on its own.

Although Rome had been withdrawing her military resources from Britain over a number of years, the exodus of the last Roman troops must have been unsettling. There are no surviving accounts to describe it, and one must look to descriptions of later evacuations to conjure what it must have been like—the marching troops tramping down the well-built Roman roads, the prancing horses of the cavalry, the exotic auxiliaries, the lumbering baggage trains, all accompanied by streams of retainers and even family retinues. Each bivouac site would have caused a local stir, the opportunity to make last sales of goods, and to have a look at the backbone of what had been the world's most powerful empire. There would have been the noisy gathering and clamor at the docks as troops and horses and massive amounts of equipment were patiently embarked onto waiting ships. Troops had come and gone before, and there must have been an expectation that they would return.

The exodus of the army did not mark the end of Roman Britain, but it did point ahead to its inevitable demise. While some towns hung on for several generations, there was general conspicuous urban decline. The villas, too, which a century before had been lavished with expensive improvements, fell into disrepair. Money was not around to be circulated; agriculture was disrupted. Deserted farm fields reverted to scrub and woodland,

LOST GOLD OF THE DARK AGES

THE MYTH OF SAXON DESTRUCTION

In the old books it was all so simple: The Romans left Britain in A.D. 410; the Britons, faced with the loss of their protectors, invited in the Anglo-Saxons, who rebelled and took over, killing most of the Britons. Now we know things were much more complicated, and a fascinating picture has emerged where even the "known unknowns" are open to question.

When did the Anglo-Saxons arrive in Britain?

The influx seems to have come around the middle of the fifth century. The late Roman army contained many Germanic soldiers, some of whom were stationed in Britain. The recruiting of Germanic soldiers likely continued, and as the Anglo-Saxons increasingly took control, more of their compatriots followed across the North Sea. During the fourth century, the Romans also sent in Germanic tribesmen as frontier guards and settlers in threatened parts of the empire, but there is no evidence that they played any part in the Anglo-Saxon takeover of Britain.

How many Germanic people migrated to Britain?

Estimates vary between the "three boat loads" (about 180 men) referred to by Gildas, the sixth-century British historian, to a mass migration that left parts of Jutland empty. The Celtic or British language died out over much of Britain and was replaced by Old English, which may suggest a large number of incomers. However, a few concentrated warriors can have a disproportionate effect, as in the case of the Arabs in Egypt. Perhaps the original influx was small and was followed by a long migration.

What happened to the Britons?

Gildas carries much responsibility for the blood-and-fire version of the Britons' fate, but a substantial number seems to have survived in Anglo-Saxon England. The Wealh (from which comes the word Welsh) people appear in Anglo-Saxon law codes. Some of the early Anglo-Saxon kings had British names (Cerdic of Wessex and Caedbaed of Lindsey). Most of the British peasants probably stayed in place, and over a few generations Old English replaced British as their language. ■

An imagined portrait of Gildas, considered Britain's earliest historian

ROMAN BRITAIN

The Romans brought stability and ended the scourge of tribal warfare in Britain. The army soon moved to the north and west, leaving much of Britain as a semiautonomous "civilian zone." Here grew several towns linked by a system of roads, and, although we see the strong influence of Roman art and culture, some objects still reflect Celtic tastes. The first to third centuries seem to have been prosperous; large numbers of small metal objects, together with imported pottery and glass, are found on rural sites, which shows that people had access to more than the basics. By the fourth century life was getting harder everywhere in the empire, although large numbers of late Roman coins suggest that Britain had an active economy in the last century of Roman rule. The following century would see all this swept away as large areas of Roman Britain became Anglo-Saxon England.

▧ Celtic-style ornamentation and the names of four forts along Hadrian's Wall adorn this colorfully enameled second-century bronze pan, which may have been commissioned as a souvenir of service by a Roman soldier.

▧ Found in a Roman cemetery at Welwyn Grange, Hertfordshire, this clay statuette of a mother goddess depicts her nursing a baby while sitting in a basketwork chair.

The graceful shape of this second-century glass jug, excavated from a grave at Bayford, Kent, is typical of Roman free-blown glass vessels. The blue-green color is natural.

Made in the Welsh tilery of the Roman army's 20th legion, whose emblem was a wild boar, this tile was set as part of an ornamental row along the eaves of a roof.

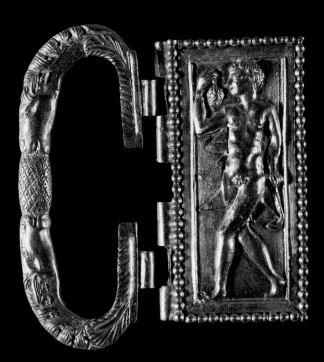

A dancing satyr enjoying a bunch of grapes adorns a gold belt buckle from Thetford, Norfolk. Created in the fourth century, the buckle shows the enduring prevalence of pagan imagery at a time when the Roman Empire was officially Christian.

Imagined by the 16th-century illustrator John White, these fanciful paintings of Pictish figures wear colorful body paint. The male brandishes a human head; the female carries a scimitar and spears.

and the land became widely forested. Decay and decline must have been everywhere apparent. The centralized factories producing pottery disappeared with the collapse of the economy and communications. One can only guess at the emotions and expectations of the remaining Romano-Britons, the people who had been shaped by three and a half centuries of Roman rule and custom. Three and a half centuries is a very long time—as historians are fond of pointing out, three and a half centuries is almost as long as the time from Shakespeare's era to our own, and far longer than the lifetime of the United States.

It is likely that different social classes viewed Rome's departure differently. For many Britons, the Roman presence may have amounted to little more than a military occupation, which they were glad to see gone, although with the army went stability and security. Surviving written accounts express regret—but these, by definition, are the products

LOST GOLD OF THE DARK AGES

of literate, educated Britons, for whom Rome meant, among other things, civilized culture. "[The Romans] had occupied the whole island south of the rampart already mentioned [Hadrian's Wall]," Bede writes, almost nostalgically, "an occupation to which the cities, lighthouses, bridges, and roads which they built there testify to this day."

The Romans' exodus would have been closely watched, and in its wake the Scotti and Picts renewed their hostilities across the now unguarded borders. That new allies from across the sea joined these old foes on occasion is clear from a reference in another source, St. Germanus of Auxerre, who made two visits to Britain on church business from Rome, in A.D. 429 and 447, and is credited by his biographer with reporting that "the Saxons and Picts had joined forces to make war upon the Britons." At the same time it seems that on both visits Germanus was traveling in a country in which vestiges of Roman infrastructure still functioned; there were men of wealth, designated meeting places in the towns, and a functioning church.

Germanus's mid-fifth-century report is the last surviving voice to come out of Britain from this critical period when so much hung in the balance. The meager written record recommences a century later with a single work—Gildas's *On the Ruin of Britain*, believed to have been written in the middle of the sixth century. Whereas Germanus departed from an island that was still, despite the barbarians pressing at the defenses, recognizably Romano-British, at least in the places he was travelling, Gildas raises the curtain on an entirely new landscape. Much of Britain is in ruins, and Gildas has the story of its downfall.

According to his account, when the barbarians in the north, joined by Saxon pirates, continued to raid the weakening former province, the Britons made one last-ditch appeal to Rome, sending a petition to one Aetius, a "powerful Roman citizen" and a consul, sometime between A.D. 446 and 454: "The barbarians drive us to the sea; the sea drives us back on the barbarians; thus two modes of death await us, we are either slain or drowned." Once again, this very last time, Rome could not comply; her own downfall in the West was only three decades away.

To whom could Britain turn? Gildas recounts the historic choice made at the initiative of a shadowy British king—a "proud tyrant"—who holds sway over a group of compliant counselors: "as a protection to their country, they sealed its doom by inviting among them like wolves into the sheep-fold, the fierce and impious Saxons, a race hateful to God and men, to repel the invasions of the northern nations." The Saxon mercenaries came in three ships—"cyuls, as they call them," Gildas notes, using the authentic Saxon term for their vessels (and the basis of the English word *keel*)—which could have carried up

LOST GOLD OF THE DARK AGES

to 180 men. At first the barbarians were generously provisioned, but then they started "to complain that their monthly supplies are not furnished in sufficient abundance, and they industriously aggravate each occasion of quarrel, saying that unless more liberality is shown them, they will break the treaty and plunder the whole island." And, according to Gildas, they were as good as their word.

"For the fire of vengeance . . . spread from sea to sea," Gildas wrote. His intent was to rebuke the Britons for their sins by drawing biblical comparisons—in this case likening the depredations of the Saxons in Briton to the Assyrians in Judea—and so one must read his descriptions with circumspection. In his telling, lofty towers topple in the streets and towers are brought low. There are shattered bodies covered with blood and houses in ruins, and those Britons who are not killed or enslaved flee to the forests, the mountains, or overseas. At length, a champion rises for the British people, one Ambrosius Aurelianus, "who of all the Roman nation was then alone in the confusion of this troubled period by chance left alive." Many scholars look wistfully to this mysterious Romano-Briton—the last of his kind, whose parents had been "adorned with the purple" (from the ruling class)—for the origin of the legend of King Arthur. Heated battles follow, with a significant victory for the British at a place called Mons Badonicus, or Mount Badon, sometime around A.D. 500. Gildas and his fellow Britons of the time, then, are living in a period of uneasy peace, albeit with the evidence of ruin around them.

Later writers including, most prominently, Bede would add details to the basic account given by Gildas. Bede states the year of the fateful invitation—circa A.D. 450—and further characterizes the Saxons: "They came from three very powerful Germanic tribes, the Saxons, Angles, and Jutes." Modern scholars, drawing on both archaeology and ancient accounts, locate the homelands of these tribes as lying in northern Germany and along the North Sea coast, Jutland and the southern Danish peninsula and islands, and Frisia, extending from northwest Holland to Denmark. The first three ships were followed, in Bede's account, by "a much larger fleet," enticed by reports of the richness of the land and "the slackness of the British." Soon, "hordes of these people eagerly crowded into the island and the number of foreigners began to increase to such an extent that they became a source of terror to the natives." The result is the bloody mayhem Gildas describes.

This lurid description of the fall of a nation is not, at face value, incredible; the annals of history contain all too many accounts of well-documented events described with comparable imagery. And to some extent archaeology substantiates Gildas's account. If there is no evidence of a Saxon invasion per se, there is much evidence that the decline that had begun even before the departure of the Romans continued apace. By around

An illustration of the Anglo-Saxon Royal Palace at Yeavering, noted in Bede's *History* as a site of Christian conversion in the seventh century

450 many cities were deserted, and evidence of organized civic life is lacking. The archaeological record indicates there was a general collapse of the population throughout Britain, although it is possible that this was caused not by Saxon raiders, but by a plague, believed to have been as potent as the Black Death, that descended on Europe at this time.

Yet as bloody as a Saxon rebellion and its aftermath may have been in specific parts of Britain, it did not spread mayhem throughout the length and breadth of the island. For a start, in the west of the island British life survived intact. Elsewhere archaeologists are finding evidence more suggestive of cultural assimilation than invasion and conquest. Excavations

at West Heslerton in Yorkshire, for example, have uncovered a sequence of settlements and villages ranging from Neolithic times to the mid-ninth century A.D., well into the Anglo-Saxon era. Most revealing is the evidence of an Anglian village established in the late fourth century, as Rome's authority was waning, but well before the bloody invasion Gildas evokes. The village and its associated cemetery slide into the evolving settlement landscape with no evidence of violence or destruction. Life lived in late Roman times, it seems, simply moved on, adapting to a new sociopolitical structure; or, to paraphrase the excavation report, by the beginning of the sixth century the population of East Yorkshire had adopted Anglian dress and burial customs, possibly brought about by the widespread availability of the material culture—not by dominance. One hears the echo of Tacitus's cynical observation: "Hence, too, a liking sprang up for our style of dress, and the 'toga' became fashionable."

As Anglo-Saxon styles and practices took hold in Britain, the old Roman ways did not vanish simultaneously, but faded at different rates. In Lincolnshire, metal detectors

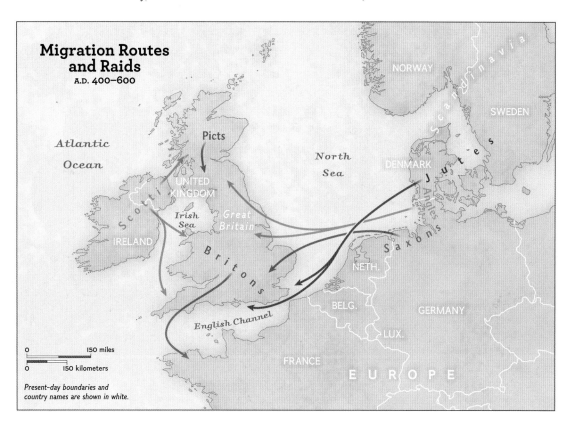

Concentric bands of
animals, based on late
Roman art, decorate this
fifth-century Anglo-Saxon
brooch from Sarre, Kent.
This style of decoration
would soon be replaced by
Anglo-Saxon designs.

have unearthed a striking number of locally made copies of late Roman military buckles; here, the inspiration for military uniforms was still evidently to some extent the Romans. Also found here, however, were German brooches from the late fourth century or early fifth century A.D. Such feminine wear suggests the presence of German families at the time Britain was still under Roman rule, suggesting in turn that Germans were stationed in Britain well before the "coming of the Saxons," possibly serving as *foederati*—allies bound to Rome by treaty—or as lower ranking *laeti*—conquered people resettled abroad.

Such artifacts, in Lincolnshire and elsewhere in Britain, do not indicate the presence of a large German contingent, let alone suggest that they turned on their hosts when their Saxon kin arrived from across the sea; rather, they are evidence of the casual diversity of Britain's population that was a legacy of the Roman occupation. The German forces may have had the kind of easy-going if controlled interaction with local people that, for example, U.S. troops stationed in Germany possess today. Possibly the average, non-elite Briton did not view the coming of the Saxons with alarm and terror. The ancient kingdom of Lindsey, which is now a part of Lincolnshire, shows almost no destruction over the transitional period from Roman to Anglo-Saxon rule. For rural workers who made up the majority of the population and who expected to live their lives under the dominance of one master or another, the transition may not have been so very disruptive. As Kevin Leahy, Anglo-Saxon authority and the leading scholar on ancient Lindsey, has memorably put it, "[F]or most people, tramping in the mud behind a plough, the view of the ox's backside remained depressingly familiar."

Whether the Germanic tribes arrived in three ships or a hundred, and whether or not they found fellow tribesmen and women in some places on their arrival, the point is that they had now come to Britain to stay. This is what made the *adventus Saxonum*—the coming of the Saxons, as the event came to be memorialized—different from all the raids with which they had plagued Gaul and Britain over the past centuries. This time, they had not come on slave raids, or to carry off portable treasure—they had come for land.

Just as the date of the adventus is in doubt, so there is question as to when the migration to Britain ended. A suggestion comes from an exotic and, at first sight, implausible source: Writing around the year A.D. 550, Procopius, a historian at the court of Justinian

FINDING THE ANGLO-SAXONS

History, archaeology, and place-names contribute to our understanding of Anglo-Saxon England. The first historical source was a diatribe on the evils of his times by the sixth-century British monk Gildas. He included, as background, a brief account of Anglo-Saxon settlement. Notes in Gallic and Byzantine records also provide some idea of events in Britain. Once the English were converted to Christianity in the seventh century, records became more common. Bede's *Ecclesiastical History* was completed in A.D. 731, and the *Anglo-Saxon Chronicle* was started in the late ninth century. Finally, the great Domesday Survey of 1086 describes England as it was in 1066 and 1086.

Archaeology is the main source for the early part of the Anglo-Saxon period. New types of pottery, brooches, and burial rites from the Germanic homelands offer evidence of incomers. Once objects were no longer placed in graves after the seventh century, this source disappeared. It is only in recent years that scholars have started to see—and understand—the middle (ca A.D. 700–870s) and later (ca 870s–1066) Saxon periods. Large-scale excavations on settlements like Flixborough, Lincolnshire, and Brandon, Suffolk, have produced large numbers of finds and evidence of middle Saxon buildings, showing the extent and richness of later Saxon society.

In England layers of place-names represent all the peoples who settled over the millennia: Celts, Romans, Anglo-Saxons, Vikings, and Normans. The survival of Celtic river names marks the extent of Anglo-Saxon settlement. In the east, where settlement was most dense, only major rivers, such as the Thames and the Trent, kept their Celtic names. In the Midlands, Anglo-Saxon settlement was less intense, with smaller streams retaining original names: the Tame, the Dove, and the Derwent. Early Anglo-Saxon settlements have names ending in -ham, such as Cleatham. Later we get -ingham place-names, like Birmingham. The common -ton place-names (Barton) appear in the eighth century. In eastern England, the Danish conquest of the later ninth century is marked by towns with names ending in -by and -thorpe: Derby and Scunthorpe. ■

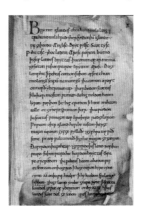

The *Anglo-Saxon Chronicle* records the history of Britain from A.D. 60 onward.

LOST GOLD OF THE DARK AGES

in Byzantium, states that on the continental shore opposite the island of Brittia, there dwell fishermen whose task is to ferry the souls of the dead over the misty water to the island. This much of the narrative does not inspire confidence, but following this fairy tale is a more interesting report:

> *Three very populous nations inhabit the Island of Brittia, and one*
> *king is set over each of them. And the names of these nations are*
> *Angles, Frisians, and Britons who have the same name as the island.*
> *So great apparently is the multitude of these peoples that every*
> *year in large groups they migrate from there with their women and*
> *children and go to the Franks.*

The "Franks," of course, are the inhabitants of Gaul, or modern France, and the migration in question—*from* Britain, *to* the Continent—is known to have occurred. The westward movement of Britons from Cornwall, in western England, and across the English Channel to what is now Brittany, in France, is well attested; Cornish and Breton, their respective languages, are today closely related. Furthermore, despite the fanciful parts of his narrative, Procopius's account of the reverse migration is substantiated by both independent German traditions and linguistic studies. Thus, by the time of his writing, about A.D. 552, the Saxon migration to Britain had stabilized; there was no more easy land—or uncontested land—to grab, and descendants of the Germanic immigrants were now looking for places to settle in continental Europe. It is also possible that they had been checked in the face of stiffening British resistance. The transforming migration to Britain, then, appears to have lasted little more than a century.

Who were the people who now inhabited Britain? Gildas states that of native Britons, all save a "miserable remnant" had fled the land or been enslaved, a claim that in this case is partly substantiated by the blunt fact that the same word—*wealh*—is used in early Anglo-Saxon law to mean both "Welshman" (i.e., Briton) and "slave." It is also true that scholars have found very little evidence of post-Roman British settlements, as opposed to those of the Anglo-Saxons, although the survival of British place-names referring to rivers and hills, or place-names referring to Britons (such as Walton or Wealh-town), suggests that certain areas may have harbored British settlements of some kind.

DNA studies of present-day Britons have produced wildly conflicting conclusions. One team of researchers reported results suggesting that Anglo-Saxon immigrants had

The Legend of Arthur

The legend of King Arthur and his kingdom of Camelot has come to denote a time when the world was pure, the spirit of man knew no bounds, and humans could accomplish great deeds. But over the centuries some scholars have thought the story might just be true.

Many historical texts mention Arthur as a great leader from the Middle Ages. The *Historia Brittonum* (ninth century A.D.) and the *Annales Cambriae* (*Welsh Annals*, tenth century A.D.) note him as a historical person of Roman descent who fought in 12 battles.

It was not until the 12th century, when French poet Chrétien de Troyes wrote a series of romances, that Arthur's name became legend. Sir Thomas Malory's *Le Morte d'Arthur* (1470) continued the legend, as did poems by Alfred, Lord Tennyson (1809–1892). Recently, leading Arthuriana

King Arthur, as pictured in a 13th-century illustration

expert Tom Green has suggested strong links between the core legend and Indo-European folk myths. Onto myth, he believes, were grafted half-remembered bits of history about the time when the British and Anglo-Saxons battled.

Other scholars have offered historical candidates to assume Arthur's mantle:

- Geoffrey of Monmouth (*History of the Kings of Britain*, 1138) believed him to be the grandson of Constantine in the fifth century.
- Geoffrey Ashe (*King Arthur's Avalon*, 1957) claimed he was King Riothamus of Brittany, who crossed the channel to fight the Visigoths in A.D. 468.
- Several studies say he is none other than Arthuis, a northern King who lived just a generation before most of the celebrated stories.
- P. F. J. Turner (*The Real King Arthur*, 1993) posits that he was the descendant of Lucius Artorius Castus, a general who commanded Roman troops in Britain.

The stories continue to enchant us, perhaps because they contain shadowy remembrances of historical fact. Perhaps Merlin's wizardry recalls the "secret knowledge" of the Druids. Perhaps Excalibur's magic properties echo ancient reverence for the "magic" of pouring molten metal into a stone mold—and pulling, as did young Arthur, a gleaming sword from the stone. ■

displaced virtually the whole British population and had pushed all the natives west to Wales; another study conducted at more or less the same time concluded that British Celts remained in both England and Ireland. More reliable than the DNA surveys are stable isotope analyses of tooth-enamel samplings taken from migration-era cemeteries; tooth enamel is formed in childhood and absorbs chemicals present in the soil and water at the time of development, a fact that in turn allows scientists to identify the geographical region of childhood. The team excavating in West Heslerton in Yorkshire,

on examining 24 skeletal remains from the early Anglian cemetery, found that only 4 of these were from Scandinavia, 10 were local to the area, and 10 came from west of the Pennine hills in northern England and southern Scotland. On the basis of burial items, the cemetery appeared to be solidly Anglian, but clearly the people who had acquired these items were mostly British born. Assimilation, not extermination, is the most likely explanation for the "disappearance" of the British population.

Of the immigrant Saxons, to use the all-purpose term most employed by ancient writers, we have a number of descriptions, albeit as observed through the watchful eyes of the Romans. "For my own part, I agree with those who think that the tribes of Germany are free from all taint of intermarriages with foreign nations, and that they appear as a

Men prepare the ground and sow grain in this Anglo-Saxon calendar dating between 1025 and 1050.

distinct, unmixed race, like none but themselves," wrote Tacitus. "Hence, too, the same physical peculiarities throughout so vast a population. All have fierce blue eyes, red hair, huge frames, fit only for a sudden exertion. They are less able to bear laborious work. Heat and thirst they cannot in the least endure; to cold and hunger their climate and their soil inure them."

For archaeologists, the Germanic immigrants are evoked most intimately by the raw data that can be culled from their cemeteries. From these we learn that the average height of men was a little over five feet eight inches and the average height of women about five feet three inches, which can be compared to the estimated average height of just under five feet seven inches for British males. Life expectancy in the early Anglo-Saxon period was, by our standards, terrifyingly short—33.1 years for women, 34.7 years for men—although consistent with that of other populations in the ancient world and also in a few parts of the modern developing world. A close study of skeletal remains from several cemeteries in Lincolnshire showed evidence of joint and spinal damage

consistent with heavy labor; but by and large, the populations appeared to have been well fed, relatively healthy, and uninjured. It is tempting to correlate the latter scientific data with the anecdotal observations of Caesar, who had wide experience of continental Germans in the course of his Gallic campaigns, and who reported that they braved the elements mostly naked, dressing only in "skins or small cloaks of deer's hides"—in other words, they were hardy folk.

The immigrants did not live in, or attempt to rebuild, the rubble of the fallen Roman towns. Their own buildings were of timber, and they lacked a tradition for working in stone. They preferred, it seems, to establish themselves on deserted sites, perhaps for practical reasons, perhaps from a desire to shun other people's ruins. The hall was the principle Anglo-Saxon residence: a single-story structure built of split timbers with a thatched gable roof and an average floor space of some 540 square feet. Roughly a quarter of these halls had a partition at one end, possibly serving as private quarters. The other characteristic structures from this early period

The gaping jaws and prominent teeth of a ship's figurehead suggest the Saxons' seafaring nature and fierceness in battle. This well-preserved figurehead dates between 400 and 615.

OPPOSITE: Seat of the Anglo-Saxon kings of Northumbria from 547 onward, Bamburgh Castle is associated with legends of King Arthur. Blurred lines of mystery, legend, and history shroud the era of Saxon rule.

are the so-called sunken-floor buildings, which were also thatched and which at one time were fancifully believed to have been hole-like dwellings in which the strapping Saxons presumably huddled Hobbit-like. Today archaeologists view them as ancillary buildings such as granaries or storage sites. A scattering of such farmsteads would make a settlement of some 12 to 50 souls. Remarkably all the settlements that have been discovered are "open," or without defensive walls, a striking fact in its own right, but especially so when compared to the hundred or so walled cities that the Romans left.

Most of these early households would have been occupied with farming and homesteading. Yet barbarian though they were, the Anglo-Saxons were well acquainted with luxury goods, intent as they had been on plundering them for some centuries. In Kent, strategically located close to the channel crossing to the Continent, it appears that silver was imported. Exotic finds such as ivory, cowrie shells, and coral from fifth- and sixth-century graves show links with Africa and the Indian Ocean. More generally, trade in a few important commodities—such as salt for preserving food and metals for tools and weapons—continued on a small scale. The Anglian settlement at West Heslerton had a craft and industry area equipped with a kiln, which shows evidence of ironwork. Slaves were traded too, it seems, along with cattle, for which London, much reduced, served as a market. More significant for our purposes, an analysis of the Staffordshire Hoard indicates that the garnets embedded in the elaborate gold cloisonné were likely from Bohemia or Portugal or even India.

Nothing in this survey of the lives and livelihoods of the Anglo-Saxon immigrants indicates how great and historic a landmark was their arrival, nor how the culture that eventually evolved not only transformed Britain but also, indirectly, left its mark on the world. And although the burial evidence suggests an assimilation of the British population within that of the Anglo-Saxon, in truth this did not represent an equal fusion of two cultures, but rather the dominance of one, the Anglo-Saxon. The evidence of this is seen most unambiguously in the Anglo-Saxons' most enduring and potent legacy—their language. Across the English Channel, much of Europe emerged from the post-Roman world speaking Romance languages—Spanish, Italian, French—based on the Latin of the now vanished Romans. In England, however, the language that defined the island was Germanic—English, or the language of the Angles. And from this point forward we may refer to the speakers of this language as the English and to the country they claimed as England.

LOST GOLD OF THE DARK AGES

Chronicle of the Anglo-Saxons

Spanning the era from the withdrawal of Roman troops in the fifth century to the Battle of Hastings in 1066, the Anglo-Saxon era was a time of conflict and cultural transformation in religion, writing, and the consolidation of power that would help give rise to modern England. The years of Saxon influence would see the large-scale conversion of England to Christianity, the introduction of English as a written language, and political advances that would shape the monarchical system.

CA A.D. 476
Angles, Saxons, and Jutes invade Britain; according to many historians, the migration of Anglo-Saxons to Britain happened continuously from A.D. 300 to 700.

CA 350–50 B.C.
Iron Age Britons make ritual sacrifices of weapons and shields in the Thames River.

A.D. 410
Goths sack Rome; Romans leave Britain.

A.D. 597
Augustine founds the Catholic Church in England and becomes the first Archbishop of Canterbury; in 601 he baptizes King Æthelberht.

55 AND 54 B.C.
Julius Caesar invades Britain.

A.D. 432
Patrick, a Christian bishop from Britain, travels to Ireland as a missionary. He sets up his diocese at Armagh and begins to convert the island to Christianity.

CA A.D. 625
Death of Raedwald, the king possibly buried at Sutton Hoo.

A.D. 43
Romans invade Britain. They eventually establish a series of forts and fortifications along the coast and northern borders of Britain.

A.D. 655
Penda of Mercia, the most powerful Saxon king of his time and founder of the Mercian supremacy, is killed at the Battle of the Winwaed in the course of a final campaign against the Bernicians.

CA A.D. 750
The epic poem *Beowulf,* considered the high point of Anglo-Saxon literature, is first written down, though it describes events from the fifth century.

A.D. 825
The period of Mercian dominance comes to an end with the defeat by Egbert of Wessex at the Battle of Ellendun.

A.D. 991
Vikings defeat Anglo-Saxons at the Battle of Maldon, which is recorded in an epic poem in Old English.

A.D. 1066
Anglo-Saxon rule comes to an end when William is crowned king following the Battle of Hastings.

CA A.D. 600-700
Probable deposit of the Staffordshire Hoard.

CA A.D. 793
Raiders and colonists from Scandinavia sack the monastery at Lindisfarne.

A.D. 878
Alfred of Wessex holds off Viking invaders and sets about massive reforms in England, including establishing a series of burghs and introducing the lingua franca of English to common use.

CHAPTER TWO

KILLING WEAPONS

"Their whole life is occupied in hunting and in the pursuits of the military art; from childhood they devote themselves to fatigue and hardships"

— JULIUS CAESAR

KILLING WEAPONS

A n inventory of the Staffordshire Hoard contained over 3,490 individual pieces, nearly half of which weighed less than a gram and included objects as small as a single bead, a glass pellet, or a rivet head. Some pieces still covered in soil were enigmatic enough to be categorized simply as "Fragment" or even "Earth lumps." The many items that could be securely identified, however, presented a striking pattern: 151 sword hilt plates, 92 sword pommel caps, 73 sword hilt collars, and 10 pyramids from sword scabbards. The majority of the miscellaneous small items—mounts and rivets, studs and helmet fragments—also appeared to be associated with weaponry. In fact, out of the entire collection, only three pieces were, in the words of the official assessment, "clearly non-martial."

A few obvious explanations come to mind as to why this hoard of carefully selected, overwhelmingly masculine, and militaristic objects was assembled. It was war plunder, perhaps, or a collection of broken weapons to be recycled into new gear. But while the hoard's purpose is mysterious, its composition is not surprising, for the Anglo-Saxons, particularly in these early, formative centuries, were, above all else, a militaristic people.

Written documentation from this period is meager to nonexistent, and we can only infer the character of English society from such archaeological evidence as burial practices and artistic motifs and written accounts of Germanic traditions of other periods and regions. It was Roman writers who first brought the Germanic tribes into sharp focus by assessing their military culture with respectful eyes. "Their whole life is

OPPOSITE: A fearsome masterpiece of Anglo-Saxon war craft, the exquisite Coppergate Helmet from York dates to the second half of the eighth century. Helmet fragments make up a portion of the Staffordshire Hoard.

PREVIOUS PAGES:
A commemorative cross marks the battlefield at Heavenfield, where King Oswald of Bernicia clashed with the Welsh in 633 or 634.

Warriors clash in this bronze matrix from sixth-century Sweden. The matrix was used in the manufacture of helmet plaques.

occupied in hunting and in the pursuits of the military art; from childhood they devote themselves to fatigue and hardships," wrote Caesar of his encounters with them in 53 B.C. Tacitus, writing at the end of the first century A.D., devotes an entire treatise—*Germania*—to a description of the country and people who then lived north of the Rhine and the Danube. They carry short, narrow swords, he notes, and their infantry also carry javelins, which they hurl "to a great distance, either naked or lightly clad in cloaks." Their battle lines are drawn in wedge formation, and for a warrior to throw away his shield is the "supreme disgrace." Leaders are attended by a cadre of companions, for whom to "outlive one's leader by withdrawing from battle brings lifelong infamy and shame."

That the Germanic warriors continued to display striking panache is apparent in a fifth-century letter written by Sidonius Apollinaris, the aristocratic future Bishop of Clermont in Gaul, describing the attendance of German chiefs at a royal wedding: "Green mantles they had with crimson borders; baldrics supported swords hung from their shoulders, and pressed on sides covered with cloaks of skin secured by brooches," he writes, betraying the kind of wary fascination that today might be extended to a cadre of gaudily arrayed professional wrestlers. "No small part of their adornment consisted of their arms: in their hands they grasped barbed spears and missile axes; their left sides were guarded by shields, which flashed with tawny golden bosses and snowy silver borders."

The most common piece of military equipment found in Anglo-Saxon burials is the wooden-shafted, iron-headed spear. Evidence suggests that the length of the spear may have been related to the age of its bearer. Legal documents tell us that only a freeman could carry a spear, and the weapon seems to have been a kind of standard-issue token of a male's right to bear arms. Tacitus, writing of the Germanic tribes of his era, remarked that on the field and off, the men were always under arms, and that when a boy came of age he was presented with a shield and spear—"the equivalent of our toga." Also a common burial item, the shield was constructed of a light wood, such as poplar or willow, covered with leather, and surmounted by an iron boss. According to Tacitus, Germanic war equipment was generally not ostentatious, but the shields, exceptionally, were "picked out in carefully chosen colours"; remains of shields in Anglo-Saxon graves indicate they were sometimes embellished with metal plates in the forms of birds and fish.

LOST GOLD OF THE DARK AGES

Spears and shields required craftsmanship to assemble, the shield boss in particular being a complex item, forged in one piece. The elite weapon, however—the apex of Teutonic military craft—was the sword and, by the sixth century, in particular the long cutting sword, a version of which the Roman cavalry had used. Averaging about three feet long and three inches wide, the sword blades were pattern welded, a sophisticated technique by which rods and strips of iron or steel were twisted and hammered together; when the blade was ground, the intricate folds and layers formed polished patterns, such as chevrons or herringbone designs. Sword hilts were sometimes adorned with metal

A medieval view of the arrival of the Anglo-Saxons in England. With its armored knights it is hopelessly inaccurate but shows the unchanging horror of battle during the time of cut-and-thrust weapons.

Axes are rare in Anglo-Saxon graves, and none were found in the Staffordshire Hoard. This ax was found in a grave in Kent and was probably imported from the Continent.

FOLLOWING PAGES: In addition to weapon parts, the Staffordshire Hoard contained a series of garnet set plates and strips, the function of which is unknown.

fittings of iron, silver, or gold, while the grips were made from wood or horn, and sometimes ivory.

An early sixth-century letter shows the widespread admiration the Teutonic sword attracted. Written on behalf of Theodoric the Great, king of the Ostrogoths, the letter thanks another Germanic king for an array of splendid gifts that had included fair-skinned slave boys and, more impressively, swords:

> *. . . swords capable even of cutting through armour, which I prize more for their iron, than for the gold upon them. So resplendent is their polished clarity that they reflect with faithful distinctiveness the faces of those who look upon them. So evenly do their edges run down to a point that they might be thought not shaped by files but moulded by the furnace. The central part of their blades . . . appear to be grained with tiny snakes, and here such varied shadows play that you would believe the shining metal to be interwoven with many colours."*

The earliest Anglo-Saxon weapon burials date from as early as the first half of the fifth century. Given that the age of males buried with weapons ranged from one to sixty years, it is unlikely that all, or even most, of the men buried with spear and sword were warriors. Probably the weapons were symbolic and few of the "warriors" may ever have wielded a sword.

Such ubiquitous tokens reveal how greatly militarism was admired and aspired to throughout every level of society. Both written testimonies and archaeology tell us, however, that the weapons themselves were not merely symbolic but also brutally functional. In an account of a killing blow wielded by Theodoric to Odovacar, rival as ruler of Italy, in 493, Theodoric "pierced Odovacar's body down to the hip." Similarly, a study of skeletons from an Anglo-Saxon cemetery in Kent provides a sobering glimpse of the damage these weapons could cause: "Male, aged 25–35 years . . . has a single linear cranial injury 16 cm long . . . the plane of the injury is almost vertically downwards"; "male aged 20–25 years . . . thirty bone injuries have been catalogued which represent a minimum of seven cranial and eleven post-cranial blows"; "male aged 35 + . . . has a single cranial injury

THE ART OF THE SWORD

The magnificent sword fittings found in the Staffordshire Hoard present only half of the story: Such fittings had been stripped from what must have been superb blades. In Anglo-Saxon England, a fine sword blade was itself a treasure. Swords were given names and bequeathed in wills. In the 11th century, Prince Æthelstan bequeathed to his brother, Edmund, a sword that was said to have belonged to Offa, the king of Mercia who died in 796. A fine blade could be fitted with a new hilt; the blades changed little, but the hilt needed to conform to the latest styles.

The making of a blade was a long process requiring considerable skill; the iron had to be smelted from its ore and beaten into narrow bars, then twisted and hammered flat. The angled lines formed by the twists were laid on a bar that would make up the blade's core. At white-hot temperatures, bars were hammered together so that they fused to form a blade. Strips of carbon steel welded onto each of its sides made edges sharp.

Once the blade had been assembled, it was ground and polished, the angled lines reappearing as patterns, and it was fitted with a hilt. The hilt of an Anglo-Saxon sword consisted of a number of elements. Top and bottom guards each contained two metal plates separated by a layer of wood, bone, ivory, or, most likely, horn. Between the guards was a grip of bone, horn, or wood. In some cases, the grip bore decorated metal rings, examples of which were found in the hoard. The hilt fittings were slipped over a tang on the blade's end, which was heated and hammered to form a button that held the elements together. This button was covered by the pommel cap, secured by four or more long rivets. Some pommel caps bore a ring, the function of which is unknown, but it may have played a part in the swearing of oaths. ■

A drawing of a blacksmith at work, from a 14th-century book of hours

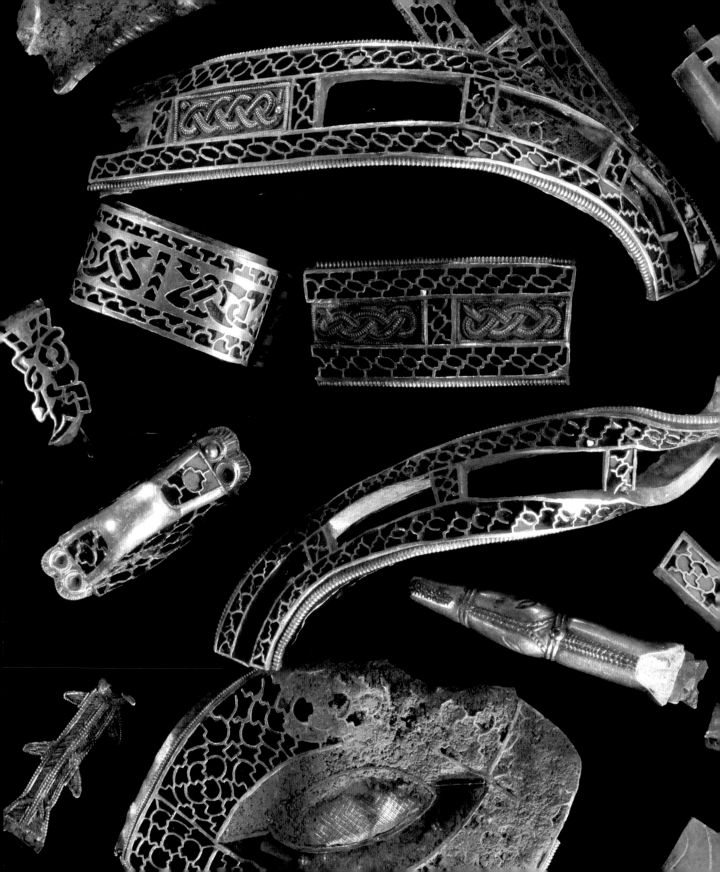

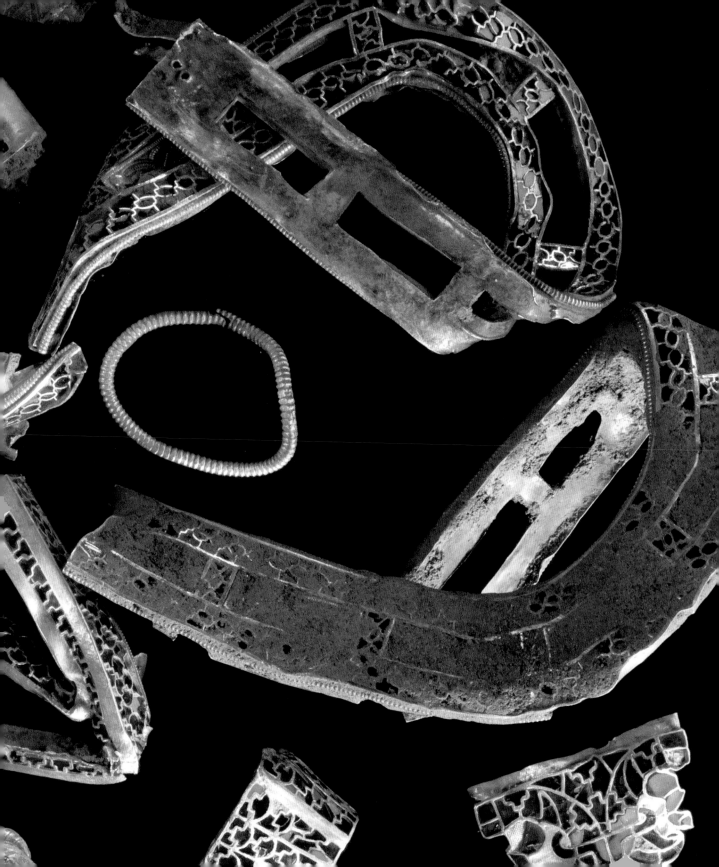

and a projectile injury to the lumbar spine. The cranial injury is to the right side of the back of the head, showing a long, curved cut on the cranial vault and two small wounds to the inner surface of the skull. The latter show that the blade passed right through the brain to contact the bone lying below it." Even the matter-of-fact catalog of wounds is painfully evocative. (A description of "experimental axe wounds" inflicted on modern cadavers by the archaeologist conducting the study, while not for the faint of heart, should give the lie to any notion that Anglo-Saxon history is a dry subject.)

The pattern of skeletal injuries tells much about the nature of the conflict that produced them. Two adversaries faced each other in single combat, each armed with shield and sword, and each exchanged blows mostly at their opponent's head, shoulders, and arms in downward strokes. Sweeping blows could be decisive but also left an opening for a counterblow; skillful use of a shield would be vital. Historically, such slashing matches had not always been recommended swordplay. Roman soldiers, for example, had been taught "not to cut but to thrust," according to a fifth-century military training manual. "A stroke with the edges, though made with ever so much force, seldom kills," while a thrusting stab is "generally fatal." Unlike the Romans, who fought in units, an Anglo-Saxon battle probably broke down into a series of single combats.

No comparable manual on the training of Anglo-Saxon warriors exists, and we must infer much from later heroic poems and sagas not only of England, but also of other northern Germanic traditions, such as those found in Scandinavia and Iceland. Germanic warriors learned to use weapons through hunting as well as specifically military drills, a fact Caesar observed as early as the first century B.C. As in many warrior societies, young men banded together for hunting, training, and also raiding and looting. A remarkable aspect of these war bands of unsettled youths, widely attested in Indo-European as well as specifically Germanic cultures, was their adoption of animal traits and identities, such as dressing in wolf skins and committing taboo acts for initiation. A die from Cambridgeshire shows the wolf-warrior was known in England. And in the *Hrafnsmál*, a ninth-century Norse poem, a raven tells a Valkyrie about the practices of warriors at King Harold's court:

Hastings, Saturday, October 14, 1066. The Bayeux Tapestry shows the traditional Anglo-Saxon shield-wall facing mounted Norman knights. The Anglo-Saxons almost won.

OPPOSITE: This rare, finely preserved coat of chain mail came from a drained lake at Illerup, Denmark. Held together by more than 20,000 rings, the coat weighed over 20 pounds.

A fragment of the eighth-century Repton Stone, a cross shaft, showing a mounted warrior, possibly King Æthelbald of Mercia, who, following his assassination in 757, was buried at Repton

Wolfcoats are they called who bear
bloodstained swords to battle;
they redden spears then they come to the slaughter,
acting together as one.

In the same tradition was the *berserkr* warrior, who fought in a frenzy, literally running berserk; the word probably refers either to the "bearshirt," or bearskin, the warrior wore or possibly to his "bare shirt," a reference to the fact that he fought naked. Depictions of barbarian warriors naked except for a belt have been found in both early Scandinavian and Roman art, and the practice has an unexpected modern parallel in the Butt Naked Brigade, a Liberian warrior gang that fought naked while terrorizing civilians during Liberia's long civil war. In both cases, the calculated act of madness represented by the warriors' nakedness and the almost supernatural confidence such nakedness manifested in the face of tearing weapons of iron and steel helped make these fearsome fighting units so effective. The berserkr warrior and the practice of war as a kind of god-sent frenzy was in sharp contrast to the dispassionate, studied professionalism of the Roman army. Victory, according to the Roman military manual cited above, is attained only by "skill and discipline" and by "continual practice" and training recruits "to every maneuver." Rome's objective had been to win and hold an empire, while the roaming barbarian Germanic tribes mostly had sought plunder; but Roman discipline ultimately fell to the barbarians.

At the head of any warrior band, disciplined or wolflike, was the lord, to whom all followers and companions pledged loyalty. Roman writers had noted this bond, and it retained its potency down the centuries and through the Anglo-Saxon age. A lord gave his companions and retainers, or thanes, valuable gifts and protection, and in return the companion was expected to give his life if called upon. Heroic poetry makes this explicit, as these lines from the late-tenth or early-eleventh-century *Battle of Maldon* make clear:

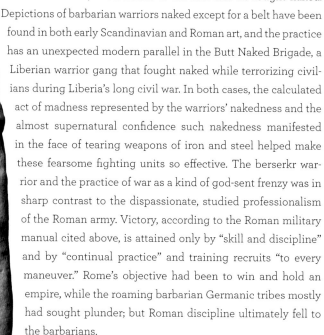

Quickly was Offa cut down in the fight;
yet he had carried out what he had promised his lord,
when he vowed to his treasure-giver
that both together should ride safely home into the stronghold,
or fall in the army,
die of wounds on the field of battle.
He lay as befits a thane, close by his lord.

Shame and infamy were the fate of any warrior who survived the death of his lord in battle; Tacitus had said as much, and in the eighth century A.D. we find the following entry in the *Anglo-Saxon Chronicle:* The thanes, or retainers, of King Cynewulf, having learned their king had been killed in an ambush, were offered "life and rewards" by his slayer if they came over to him—"which none of them would accept, but continued fighting together against him, till they all lay dead."

A mounted warrior tramples a fallen enemy in this detail from the seventh-century battle helmet from Sutton Hoo. This motif is well known and occurs on some of the silver foils from the Staffordshire Hoard.

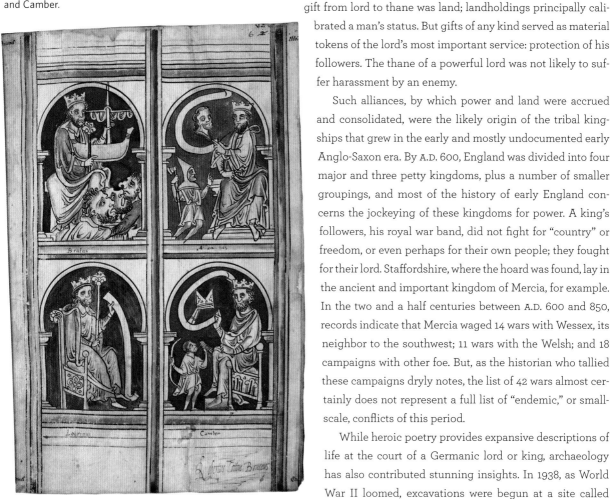

This central bond of Anglo-Saxon society was, then, a highly practical arrangement. It was also, at least in poetic sagas, emotional, and a thane who had lost his lord was like a man without a home, an exile from society.

"[L]ong ago earth covered my lord in darkness," mourns the speaker of the tenth-century poem *The Wanderer*, "and I, wretched, thence, mad and desolate as winter, over the wave's binding sought, hall-dreary, a giver of treasure." The exile "remembers hall-warriors and treasure-taking," and how "his gold-friend," or lord, "received him at the feast."

Heroic poetry is replete with gifts of gold and weapons, but historically a common gift from lord to thane was land; landholdings principally calibrated a man's status. But gifts of any kind served as material tokens of the lord's most important service: protection of his followers. The thane of a powerful lord was not likely to suffer harassment by an enemy.

Such alliances, by which power and land were accrued and consolidated, were the likely origin of the tribal kingships that grew in the early and mostly undocumented early Anglo-Saxon era. By A.D. 600, England was divided into four major and three petty kingdoms, plus a number of smaller groupings, and most of the history of early England concerns the jockeying of these kingdoms for power. A king's followers, his royal war band, did not fight for "country" or freedom, or even perhaps for their own people; they fought for their lord. Staffordshire, where the hoard was found, lay in the ancient and important kingdom of Mercia, for example. In the two and a half centuries between A.D. 600 and 850, records indicate that Mercia waged 14 wars with Wessex, its neighbor to the southwest; 11 wars with the Welsh; and 18 campaigns with other foe. But, as the historian who tallied these campaigns dryly notes, the list of 42 wars almost certainly does not represent a full list of "endemic," or small-scale, conflicts of this period.

While heroic poetry provides expansive descriptions of life at the court of a Germanic lord or king, archaeology has also contributed stunning insights. In 1938, as World War II loomed, excavations were begun at a site called

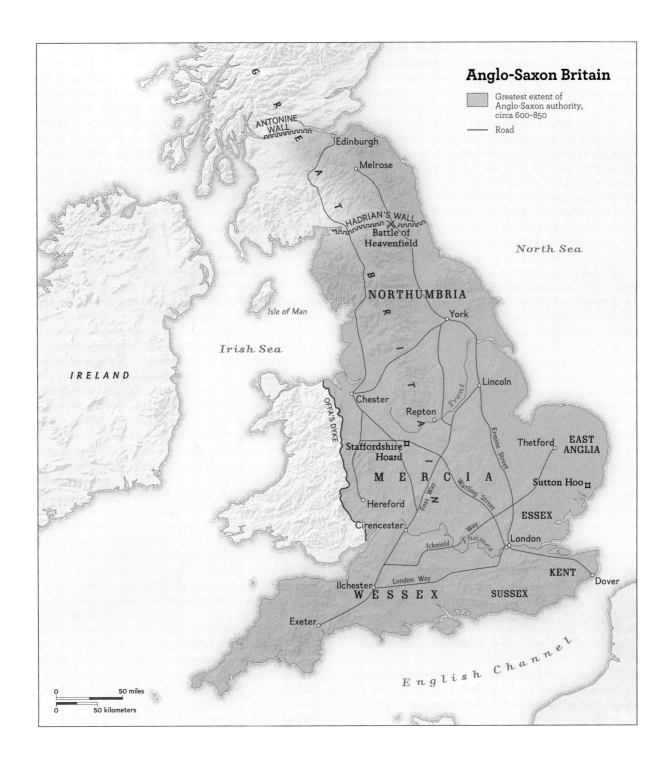

Anglo-Saxon Britain

Greatest extent of
Anglo-Saxon authority,
circa 600–850

——— Road

ANTONINE
WALL

Edinburgh

Melrose

G R E A T

HADRIAN'S WALL

Battle of
Heavenfield

North Sea

NORTHUMBRIA

Isle of Man

York

Irish Sea

Lincoln

Chester

IRELAND

Trent

Repton

Ermine Street

EAST
ANGLIA

Thetford

OFFA'S DYKE

Staffordshire
Hoard

M E R C I A

Sutton Hoo

Hereford

Foss Way

Watling Street

ESSEX

Cirencester

Icknield

Way

Thames

London

KENT

Ilchester

London Way

Dover

W E S S E X

SUSSEX

Exeter

English Channel

0   50 miles

0   50 kilometers

Engraved with the names of Anglo-Saxon rulers, these ninth-century rings may have been royal gifts or symbols of office.

FOLLOWING PAGE: The eighth-century crypt in St. Wystan's Church in the village of Repton, Derbyshire, held the remains of the murdered Prince Wystan, thought to have miraculous power.

Sutton Hoo, on a bluff overlooking the River Deben in Suffolk, where a cluster of conspicuous barrows or mounds had long attracted attention. The first mounds excavated proved to have been robbed during the Elizabethan age, but the largest of the mounds contained what is now regarded as one of the archaeological treasures of England: the burial of a warrior king of East Anglia, from the early seventh century A.D. Here, in the royal grave where they had been laid well over a thousand years earlier, were the physical objects evoked in the heroic songs: a stone scepter surmounted by a regal bronze stag; a hanging bowl embellished with Celtic patterns of colored glass; bowls, dishes, spoons of fine silver, an iron ax, and a pattern-welded sword; a drinking horn and gold buckle of fabulous intricacy; the remains of a coat of chain mail and relics of leather and woven clothing; and an iron helmet resembling a mask that is so distinctive and striking it has become the iconographic image of the Anglo-Saxon age.

Most stunning of all, these splendid objects were assembled in the belly of what had been a wooden ship. Although the wood, like the bones of the royal warrior it held, had disintegrated long ago, it had a left a ghostly imprint in the sand, an eerie impression of gunwales and strakes studded with the surviving iron rivets. At almost 90 feet in length and just under 15 feet in width, the Sutton Hoo vessel was almost twice the size of the only other ship burial found in England—that at Snape, only nine miles away.

> *Scyld was still thriving when his time came*
> *and he crossed over into the Lord's keeping.*
> *His warrior band did what he bade them*
> *when he laid down the law among the Danes:*
> *they shouldered him out to the sea's flood,*
> *the chief they revered who had long ruled them.*
> *A ring-whorled prow rode in the harbour,*
> *ice-clad, outbound, a craft for a prince.*
> *They stretched their beloved lord in his boat,*
> *laid out by the mast, amidships,*
> *the great ring-giver. Far-fetched treasures*
> *were piled around him, and precious gear.*
> *I never heard before of a ship so well furbished*
> *with battle tackle, bladed weapons*
> *and coats of mail.*
> *Beowulf, 26–40*

Saxon Warriors and Gear

Anglo-Saxon England was a martial society, more so than those on the Continent. The chronicles record almost constant warfare, with the Anglo-Saxons fighting the Welsh, the Vikings, and very often each other. The most common weapon was the spear, which early law codes show could only be carried by free men. Excavators have found iron bosses from the centers of wooden shields, but rarely swords and helmets. Body armor is almost unknown; the mail shirt from the Sutton Hoo ship burial is the sole example. Bequests in later Saxon wills, however, suggest that it was not uncommon.

Not everyone buried with weapons was a warrior; in some cases the person in the grave was too young or infirm to have made use of them. There is some evidence that men buried with weapons were slightly taller than those without, perhaps indicating a warrior elite. But male bones found with spearheads show the men to have suffered all the ills of brutal work; these were farmers tilling the land, not a pampered aristocracy. Oddly, weapons are less common in graves during times of war than in more peaceful times. Perhaps during conflict people had better things to do with weapons than burying them, or active warriors had already shown their military prowess. Dressing up has always been an important aspect of warfare: Splendid equipment boosts a man's ego and daunts his enemies. The superb objects found in the Staffordshire Hoard surely would have been carried in battle; a warrior had to show his status, and it would have been unthinkable to hide it behind plain clothing. Although we know little about Anglo-Saxon beliefs regarding life after death, we do know that they wanted to be remembered. The duty of caretaking memories of heroic deeds traditionally fell to poets, such as Homer in times past and the anonymous author of *Beowulf*, who would tell and retell the tales, thus preserving them for the ages. ∎

Faces of warriors adorn this fragment of silver foil, which may have decorated a helmet.

Much as the discovery of the ruins of Troy on the Dardanelles had made the *Iliad* and its story of the Trojan War real, so the discovery of the Sutton Hoo burial made the heroic world of the Anglo-Saxon warriors tangible and historic. The finds also confirmed the remarkable commonality of culture between the Germanic settlers of England and their kin in Scandinavia. The poem *Beowulf,* uncertainly dated to somewhere between the mid-seventh and early tenth century, also straddles the heroic cultures of these two people: The poem is written in the Anglo-Saxon language—and is, then, in Old English—but it is set in Scandinavia, and Beowulf himself is the warrior-hero of the Geats in southern Sweden. Similarly, the counterparts to the ship at Sutton Hoo are the pre-Viking burial ships found in Sweden, while the specifically Swedish character of a number of the Sutton Hoo objects has led to speculation that the East Anglian dynasty to which the buried king belonged might have been of Swedish ancestry.

While much is known about particular aspects of Anglo-Saxon warfare and weaponry, much remains unknown about how these different features were assembled. Was a war-band, or *fyrd,* for example, composed only of the nobility? Or did peasants also participate as warriors? How was fyrd service levied? A late-seventh-century law code cites fines imposed for neglected military service, but it is unclear if this was a standing law or a measure established in reaction to a specific local threat. How large were the armies? Estimates range from a few thousand men to an improbable 20,000. And tactically, how were wars fought? Did warriors fight, as well as travel, on horseback? The motif of a spear-wielding warrior riding a horse as he runs down a hapless foe adorns the iron helmet found in the royal burial at Sutton Hoo and also appears in the Staffordshire Hoard—but these scenes may be mythological or even classical, not realistic. Given that horses of this era in Britain stood only eight to ten hands high, about the size of a Shetland pony, warhorses would have to have been specially bred. Probably, the early army was not divided into cavalry or infantry, and a warrior fought on foot or horse as circumstances required. Shield maids, or women warriors, are well attested in poetic traditions. Did they have counterparts on the historical field of war?

LEFT AND BELOW: Gold and garnet hilt fittings from the Sutton Hoo ship burial, together with a modern re-creation of its superb pattern-welded blade

OPPOSITE: The reconstructed ceremonial helmet from the seventh-century Sutton Hoo ship burial in Suffolk is remarkable for its face mask and decorative motifs of interlacing animals and heroic scenes.

The Sutton Hoo ship burial complements the Staffordshire Hoard and fills out its background. At Sutton Hoo not only the jewels and the ship were found, but everything else that an Anglo-Saxon king would need for the afterlife.

FOLLOWING PAGES: A sunset casts into relief the Sutton Hoo burial mound in Suffolk.

The price of war in Anglo-Saxon times was, as now, high, and death in battle was the common fate of the warrior king. Of 22 battles recorded in the seventh century, 12 saw the death of "at least one royal figure." A good king was by necessity also a good warlord. The Sutton Hoo warrior, buried with his magnificent sword and shield, may have been King Raedwald, known to have died around A.D. 624, "shortly after the battle of Idle," according to Bede. How he died is not known, and his bones have not survived to tell us; the *Anglo-Saxon Chronicle*, however, tells of his association with a royal death by noting that in the year 617, "Æthelfrith king of the Northumbrians [was] slain by Raedwald, king of the East-Angles."

A royal burial like that at Sutton Hoo, along with the more humble cremations and burials found in Anglo-Saxon cemeteries throughout England, tells of the inevitable

SOCIAL CLASSES

While many basic aspects of Anglo-Saxon society remained unchanged over the centuries, people became wealthier. When we look at finds from fifth- and sixth-century graves, some are richer than others, but none is outstanding; few, if any, could be considered aristocratic. In the seventh century, however, although most burials contain little in the way of grave goods, a few are exceedingly rich, with gold and garnet jewelry and swords, likely indicating the rise of an aristocracy. The Staffordshire Hoard must represent the upper aristocracy, its treasure belonging to the king and his companions.

Slavery was common in Anglo-Saxon England. In the Domesday Survey of 1086, slaves formed about 10 percent of the population; most were agricultural laborers but occasionally also skilled workers. Slavery declined in the late Saxon period and disappeared after the Norman Conquest. The rest of the population was graded by their *weregilds*—the fines payable for killing them. This system was intended to allow disputes to be settled and to avoid blood feuds. Everyone, including the king, had a value, and these values varied with time and place. In seventh-century Wessex, a nobleman was valued at 1,200 shillings and a free peasant at 200 shillings, with an intermediate grade at 600 shillings. A murdered woman was valued at her father's, rather than her husband's, weregild, and, if she was pregnant, her unborn child had half its father's value. King Alfred divided his subjects into those who prayed, those who fought, and those who toiled. Those who prayed ranged from great prelates like St. Wilfrid to poor country priests; those who fought included both the noble earls and the common foot soldiers; and the laborers included both agricultural workers and fine craftsmen. Women who prayed included royal abbesses. Although we know of no female warriors, there were women like Aethelflaed, the Lady of the Mercians, at whose command the Vikings were driven out of the English Midlands. And the superb textile-working skills of Englishwomen were famed throughout Europe. ▪

Justice: A king and his entourage observe a hanging in this illustration from an Old English Hexateuch.

One of the most famous instances of the ritual "killing" of weapons, this image from a medieval French text shows Sir Bedivere throwing Excalibur into the lake at the dying King Arthur's command.

OPPOSITE: Weapons and personal artifacts were among the more than 15,000 Iron Age objects dating to between A.D. 200 and 400 recovered from the mud when a lake at Illerup, Denmark, was drained in 1950. It is believed they may have been deposited in a ritual sacrifice by victors in battle.

end of all warriors. More intriguing is the fate of the weapons themselves. Sometimes a fine sword, and presumably the good fortune it had won its previous owner, was passed on as a family heirloom until it was eventually buried with its final owner. A sword given to a retainer by a lord, possibly with other war equipment such as arms or even horses, represented a legal contract of sorts—the *heriot,* or "war gear," which was to be repaid to the lord if the retainer "fell before his lord." In a will written in the tenth century, a royal official bequeaths "to my royal lord as a heriot four armlets of . . . gold, and four swords and eight horses, four with trappings and four without, and four helmets and four coats-of-mail and eight spears and eight shields."

But sometimes weapons were buried without warriors, in what seems to have been a religious practice. Most evidence comes from rivers and bogs in Scandinavia, where it appears that weapons had been collected after a battle and, along with miscellaneous domestic objects, left as ritual offerings. A number of the sword blades in these deposits had been deliberately bent back and effectively broken. Similarly, deposits of weapons have been found in pools of water in both Scandinavia and Anglo-Saxon England; one Scandinavian lake sacrifice included 56 long swords, each bent and defaced. In England, the practice is also found as early as the Celtic Bronze and Iron Age.

The "killing" of swords and other weapons is an ancient tradition found in many cultures: For example, killed weapons have been found in Israel dating from the 11th century B.C., and similar weapons have been found in Dark Age Greece. Why this practice occurred is unclear; possibly it was to ensure that a warrior's weapon would never be wielded by another man's hand. Possibly the weapon was killed so as to accompany the dead warrior to the land of the dead, in the way that favorite dogs or horses were sometimes sacrificed on the pyre of their owner. Perhaps the weapons were left or buried as offerings to patron deities, and the defacing of the weapon represented the owner's complete and inexorable surrender of its use.

These facts return us to our talisman, the Staffordshire Hoard, which consisted mostly of broken military equipment. Were the weapons simply broken for easier disposal? Or had they been ritually killed before being buried in the Staffordshire ground?

CHAPTER THREE

THE BATTLE
FOR THE SOUL

*"The Gallic tribes as a whole
are slaves of superstition"*
— JULIUS CAESAR

THE BATTLE FOR THE SOUL

OPPOSITE: Created by monks around A.D. 800, the magnificently illuminated Book of Kells is probably a product of Iona. The introductory page of the Gospel of St. Matthew shows Christ surrounded by motifs that drew on both Celtic and Anglo-Saxon art.

PREVIOUS PAGES: Erected in the ninth century, the magnificent St. Martin's Cross is one of the many treasures of Iona Abbey, one of the oldest and most important religious centers in western Europe.

O f the many objects in the Staffordshire Hoard, the only items that appear to be clearly nonmartial are two gold crosses and a strip of gold inscribed with a biblical verse. One of the crosses, a pendant, may have been a part of ecclesiastic dress. The larger cross, "suited for use as an altar or processional cross," according to the preliminary report, had been crumpled and folded in the same manner as the mutilated military equipment. Also folded—bent almost in two—is the strip of gold bearing a belligerent, and misspelled, inscription from the Latin Bible, Numbers 10:35: *"surge d[omi]ne [et] disepentur inimici tui et fugent qui oderunt te a facie tua"* ("Rise up, O Lord, and may Thy enemies be scattered and those who hate Thee flee from Thy face").

How or why did these religious icons come to be gathered into a martial assemblage? In one respect, their presence amid the pagan iconography and images is appropriate, being emblematic of the jumble of religious beliefs that characterized this formative and transforming age. Christianity had first come to Britain during the Roman occupation, then faded as the Roman presence faded, and eventually was reintroduced by missionaries from the Continent and Ireland—the Irish Church in particular being a vigorous center of missionary activity. At the same time pagan beliefs of different peoples still survived. The Romans had imported the Greco-Roman pantheon as well as Christianity, and the Saxons brought with them their own northern gods—all of which were underlain by the very ancient worship and beliefs of the native Britons. Viewed

THE BATTLE FOR THE SOUL

from the safe distance of many centuries, the early Anglo-Saxon age, when the Staffordshire Hoard was buried, can be seen as a time of momentous change as Roman Christianity replaced both paganism and Celtic Christianity; and yet this mystical age also left relics of its older faiths in words and practices still in use today.

A survey of England's competing and often intermingling faiths casts some light on the composition and possible ritual character of the hoard. The beliefs of the people who inhabited the island first, however—namely, the native Britons or Celts—are the least known, and such records as there are were often written by hostile outsiders. Magic, enchantresses, and nature worship waft seductively through these accounts, along with ritual deposition and human sacrifice, but the piecemeal testimonies make it difficult to reconstruct a coherent belief system.

"The Gallic tribes as a whole are slaves of superstition," wrote Caesar. He was referring specifically to the Druids, the mysterious priestly caste whom he encountered in Gaul, but whose institution, or doctrine (*disciplina*) was "supposed to have been devised in Britain, and to have been brought over from it into Gaul; and now those who desire to gain a more accurate knowledge of that system generally proceed thither for the purpose of studying it."

As Caesar indicates, Druids were made, not born, and women as well as men trained in Britain to learn the "profession," which, according to Caesar, entailed learning "by heart a great number of verses; accordingly some remain in the course of training twenty years. Nor do they regard it lawful to commit these to writing." Caesar attributed the taboo against writing to a desire for secrecy and the concern that disciples might "devote themselves the less to the efforts of memory . . . since it generally occurs to most men, that, in their dependence on writing, they relax their diligence in learning thoroughly, and their employment of the memory." This determination to rely on oral instruction accounts in great part for the frustrating lack of documentation of this fascinating and mysterious sect. Today, the Druids are probably the most famous, if misrepresented, relic of native British religion. Popularly regarded as standing somewhere between priests and wizards, they were most likely an elite and learned class of British society, venerated as judges and scholars as well as priests.

From such varied evidence as Roman testimonies, comparison with other Celtic traditions, and British archaeological remains and place-names linked to old deities, it is possible to glimpse the spiritual world enjoyed by the Britons before the coming of

This large gold altar or processional cross, damaged in much the same way as the rest of the Staffordshire Hoard, raises many questions about the evolution of religious practices and the role of Christianity during the Saxon period.

LOST GOLD OF THE DARK AGES

Romans or Saxons. According to Caesar, a central belief was that "souls do not become extinct, but pass after death from one body to another, and they think that men by this tenet are in a great degree excited to valor, the fear of death being disregarded." Caesar attributes the belief in immortality specifically to the Druids, but this was a broader Celtic concept—and possibly the earliest manifestation in Europe—and we can assume it was also held by Celts in Britain.

Similarly, the Britons, like Celts on the Continent, made use of timber structures set within ditched enclosures but conducted most worship outside. According to Roman sources, the Druids venerated groves of trees—particularly oak—and the word *Druid* is

Long before the Romans or the Saxons, Stonehenge was a site of religious significance set within a ritual landscape. Each generation has interpreted the monument in its own way. To the Georgians it was a Druidic temple, and more recently was seen as an astronomical computer. To the Anglo-Saxons it was "stone henge," from *hengen,* a gallows.

Mars, the Roman god of war, is depicted on this bronze statuette. An inscription on its pedestal shows that although it was commissioned by a Briton, the man who made it had a Roman name.

thought to mean "knowledge of the oak." Pliny the Elder, writing in the first century A.D., states that the Druids performed "none of their religious acts without employing branches of" this sacred tree, as they believed that anything growing on the oak had been "sent immediately from heaven"—hence their veneration for the oak-borne mistletoe. These pleasing pastoral images of shadowy groves, however, are cast in a more sinister light by Roman accounts, from Caesar to the poetry of Lucan, quoted below:

> A grove there was, untouched by men's hands
> from ancient times, whose interlacing boughs enclosed
> a space of darkness and cold shade, and banished the
> sunlight far above. No rural Pan dwelt there, no
> Silvanus, ruler of the woods, no Nymphs; but gods
> were worshipped there with savage rites, the altars
> were heaped with hideous offerings, and every tree
> was sprinkled with human gore. On those boughs
> —if antiquity, reverential of the gods, deserves any
> credit—birds feared to perch; in those coverts wild
> beasts would not lie down; no wind ever bore down
> upon that wood, nor thunderbolt hurled from black
> clouds; the trees, even when they spread their
> leaves to no breeze, rustled of themselves. Water,
> also, fell there in abundance from dark springs.
> The images of the gods, grim and rude, were uncouth
> blocks formed of felled tree-trunks. Their mere
> antiquity and the ghastly hue of their rotten timber
> struck terror; men feel less awe of deities worshipped
> under familiar forms; so much does it increase
> their sense of fear, not to know the gods whom
> they dread.

Lucan's poetic account is deliberately atmospheric, but that Druids performed sacrifices of human beings is not in doubt; skeletal remains found at the bottoms of pits, in bogs, and even in granaries offer compelling evidence. The famous Lindow Man, whose body was found preserved in a bog in Cheshire, is thought to have been the victim of ritual killing in the first or second century A.D. With his manicured nails and neatly trimmed moustache and beard, he was a man of some status, but he had been struck on the head, had had a rib broken by a blow, had been strangled, and had had his throat cut before being consigned to the bog.

The Druids venerated not only groves, but also springs, lakes, and water in all forms. In Britain, as well as on the Continent, archaeologists have found the remains of ancient wooden piers or jetties that extended over water and led to deposits of domestic objects and war gear. A number of conspicuously high-quality weapons, such as the exquisite Battersea Shield, have been dredged from the Thames and other English rivers such as

Believed to have been killed in a ritual sacrifice, Lindow Man was discovered in an extraordinary state of preservation in a peat bog in northwestern England.

FOLLOWING PAGES: The Staffordshire Hoard was found on the edge of Cannock Chase, a wide expanse of forest. Three miles down Watling Street the Roman town of Letocetum took its name from the "Grey Wood." Woods are strange, alien places, hallowed in many religions, but never places of ease.

The ornate Battersea Shield, made between circa 200 and 50 B.C., was cast into the River Thames as a sacrifice.

OPPOSITE: In Bath, Victorian-era statues watch over the 2,000-year-old Roman baths, rediscovered below street level in the 1800s.

the Trent and Witham. This Celtic practice may be reflected in one of the most famous stories in the legend of King Arthur—the dramatic return of Arthur's sword Excalibur to the Lady of the Lake as he lay dying; having served its warrior owner well, the magic sword was ritually retired to the water. (As a fascinating footnote, in recent times the Thames has yielded numerous Hindu votive offerings, placed in the river by Indian immigrants, perhaps with the hope that their gifts would be borne to a place where the river's waters mingle with the sacred Ganges.)

Offerings were not only made in water. According to Caesar, following a victory the Celts would sacrifice to the god of battle "whatever captured animals may have survived the conflict, and collect the other things into one place. In many states you may see piles of these things heaped up in their consecrated spots; nor does it often happen that any one, disregarding the sanctity of the case, dares either to secrete in his house things captured, or take away those deposited; and the most severe punishment, with torture, has been established for such a deed." We will return to such ritual hoards in Chapter Five.

Rome seized on the dark stories of human sacrifice as an excuse to persecute the politically as well as spiritually powerful Druids—who, not incidentally, had been associated with native British rebellions against Roman rule. By the time the Saxons arrived, Druidism appears to have been all but dead in Britain, save for a possible relic that survived briefly amid the Picts in Scotland. But some British beliefs and practices may have survived in different degrees, and indeed the Romans strategically supported local native cults by linking native gods with the classical pantheon and adding architecture and altars of their own at important sites. Famously, the Roman resort of Bath, for example, built on hot springs held sacred by the British, was dedicated to "Sulis Minerva," a neat combination of an ancient Celtic water goddess with Rome's own Minerva.

Following the edict of Milan in A.D. 313, which proclaimed religious tolerance, the Roman Empire became increasingly Christian, and by the end of the fourth century the British population too was Christian. When the Romans departed Britain, they left their churches and towns to partial and then total abandonment. The Anglo-Saxon newcomers generally chose to build their settlements anew in fresh sites rather than attempting to renovate the rubble of buildings left by the Romans. Over time these neglected ruins were seen, through poetic eyes at least, to be dignified and melancholy reminders of the forgotten Roman age:

Carved with scenes from Roman, Jewish, Christian, and Germanic religious traditions and featuring both runes and Latin letters, this early eighth-century lidded whalebone box is known as the Auzon (or Franks) Casket. Its main inscription is an alliterative verse about its origin.

Wondrous is its wall-stone,   laid waste by the fates.
The burg-steads are burst,   broken the work of the giants.
The roofs are in ruins,   rotted away the towers.

The specific subject of this elegiac poem, "The Ruin," composed in the eighth century, is believed to be the ruins of Bath, but such nostalgic wonderment undoubtedly extended to other ruined town and cityscapes. The Germanic newcomers were no strangers to Roman customs or religion—many had served in the Roman army, after all—but confrontation with such haunting physical evidence of collapse must have been sobering.

Little unambiguous physical evidence remains of the Anglo-Saxons' own sites of worship, although later Christian writers, such as Bede, make reference to pagan altars and temples that were presumably built in perishable wood. King Raedwald, for example (whose burial, it is thought, was found at Sutton Hoo), torn as he was between Christianity and his ancestral faith, had in the same temple "one altar for the Christian sacrifice and another small altar on which to offer victims to devils."

The earliest description of Germanic worship indicates that, like that of the Celts, it was conducted in the outdoors. Tacitus, in his account of Germanic tribes on the Continent, writes that they do not "deem it consistent with the divine majesty to imprison their gods within walls or represent them with anything like human features. They consecrate woods and groves, and they call by the names of gods the hidden presence that they see only by the eye of reverence." Anglo-Saxon terms embedded in English place-names still in use today suggest that the earliest English continued their traditional rites in the open; *leah* or *ley*, a grove or clearing, for example, appears as a suffix of many names, such as Thundersley, in Essex, from *Þunres leah*—grove or clearing of Thunor (Thor); or Whiligh, in Sussex; Weeley, in Essex; and Willey, in Surrey—all meaning the grove of the *wig* or *wih*, the Anglo-Saxon word for "idol."

According to Tacitus, white horses believed to be prophetic by virtue of their closeness to the gods were kept in sacred groves "at public expense" (*publice aluntur*). Elsewhere he describes how a priest may on a "public occasion" (*si publice consuletur*) read omens made from strips of a branch of wood (there is no mention of priestesses, but according to Tacitus, "they believe that there resides in women something holy and prophetic"). Such scattered references—to publicly maintained holy sites, priests in public assembly, altars, and temples—indicate a formal, structured religion, even if it has left no physical trace.

As in other heroic societies, the Germanic tribes placed great emphasis on the survival of a warrior's reputation after death, achieved by his memorable feats in his lifetime and society's safeguarding of his memory through passing generations. For this reason scholars believe that the Anglo-Saxons, particularly with their strong sense of kinship, would have venerated their ancestors—and possibly elevated them over time to the status of gods. Such a heroic outlook is generally intent on deeds of this world, with little

The Saxon god Wotan, known in Britain as Woden, is depicted in this ink drawing sketched by Karl Rickelt in 1882.

This intricately carved buckle was recovered from Sutton Hoo. The decoration looks like knotted ribbons, but it consists of intricately intertwined animals showing the Anglo-Saxon love of riddles, both verbal and visual.

confidence in much occurring in the next. In a famous passage, Bede recounts a parable spoken by a counselor to the Northumbrian king who was considering converting to Christianity: While winter rages without, the court enjoys the warmth and light of the fire inside their lighted hall, "and a sparrow flies swiftly through the hall. It enters at one door and quickly flies out through the other . . . it flits from your sight, out of the wintry storm and into it again. So this life of man appears but for a moment; what follows or indeed what went before, we know not at all."

The point of the parable, in Bede's presentation, was that Christianity could provide "more certain information" about the dark spaces that bracket human life. This implies that survival of the soul was a novel concept to the heathen king and courtiers. Did the early English, then, have no conception of an afterlife—or was this a Christian misattribution to heathen "limitations"? Without texts or documents for guidance, one must look to the archaeological record. In the roughly 1,200 Anglo-Saxon cemeteries that have been found, grave goods are common; their purpose, however, is often unclear. The many weapons found in Anglo-Saxon graves seem to have been tokens of the deceased's status, not implements to be carried into the afterlife. But a miscellany of small burial items, such as animal teeth, cowrie shells, rock crystals, Roman coins, and even sea urchins, would appear to consist of amulets of some kind. We do not know how these functioned, however, or whether their purpose was to protect survivors from magic associated with death or the deceased on his journey.

The magnificent ship burial at Sutton Hoo appears designed to take its occupant on a momentous final voyage; yet this is uncertain, and it is possible the ceremonial ships served some other purpose. Later northern traditions tell of "ghosts," not as insubstantial will-o'-the-wisp apparitions, but as the reanimated dead. Scholars speculate that Anglo-Saxons may have held a similar kind of belief—a limited survival of sort after death, but not involving the separation, let alone freeing, of the soul from the body.

While it is impossible to determine what the Anglo-Saxons believed about life after death or the nature of the soul before the influence of Christianity, it is possible to glean threads of their more mundane preoccupations. Old riddles, medical works, poems, Christian writings, words, place-names, and archaeological finds all preserve shards of early English superstitious beliefs. A medley of four, now bizarre, elements characterized Germanic medical remedies—flying venoms,

CONVERSIONS

As pagan Anglo-Saxons moved into Britain after the Romans, Celtic Christians retreated westward or were absorbed into the invaders' Germanic culture. It was only with the advent of Christian missionaries, primarily monks from Ireland and the Continent, that the heart of England became Christian again. Thanks to the efforts of a number of strong and enlightened churchmen, many of whom were sainted, the island was converted peacefully.

St. Patrick was born about 387 to a Roman Christian family in Britain, but as a teen he was carried off to Ireland as a slave. Eventually he escaped and made his way to France, where he became a priest. Patrick returned to Britain to fight heresy and in 433 received the blessing of the pope in Rome to go to Ireland to convert the pagans. His arrival was marked by miracles, but the Irish did not begin to convert until an Easter fire that Patrick lit near the royal hill of Tara could not be extinguished.

Since Ireland converted before Anglo-Saxon England, Irish missionaries were instrumental in many English conversions. St. Aidan was an Irish bishop who went to Iona as a monk around 630. In 635 the king of Northumbria summoned Aidan to the island of Lindisfarne, where he established a monastery similar to Iona. Lindisfarne, or Holy Island, educated religious men, produced bishops and missionaries, and founded churches across northern England.

St. Theodore of Tarsus from Asia Minor was appointed Archbishop of Canterbury in 668 at the age of 66. When he arrived in England for the first time a year later, he changed the English Church forever. Theodore's genius was management and teaching. He toured the English dioceses and redistricted them or founded new ones based on what served the religious population best. He consecrated more bishops and established a school in Canterbury—the King's School, now the oldest in England—that taught Christians of both Roman and Celtic traditions. Much of his redistricting remains intact to this day. ■

St. Cuthbert and two of the brethren sail to the land of the Picts to convert them to Christianity.

the number nine, the worm, and elves. "If a horse or other cattle is shot, take dock seed and Scottish wax and let a man sing twelve masses over them," advises Bald's *Leechbook,* a medical compilation dating from around 950. "Elf-shot," the invisible arrows launched by evil-minded elves (not all were bad), was of particular concern, to judge by the many remedies to counteract its harm to man, animals, and even fields.

Typically the clearly Germanic elements of these charms and herbal remedies appear amid a tangle of biblical or Christian imagery, as in the case of an incantation, undoubtedly older than the A.D. 1000 manuscript in which it was preserved:

> *A serpent came crawling (but) it destroyed no one*
> *When Woden took nine twigs of glory*
> *(and) then struck the adder so that it flew into nine (pieces).*
> *There achieved apple and poison*
> *That it never would re-enter the house.*
> *Chervil and Fennel, very powerful pair . . .*

The old Germanic gods, known from later Scandinavian mythology, can also be located in the English landscape and language: Tiw, a god of rules and order in both government and battle; Woden (Germanic Wotan, Viking Odin), the warrior and hunter; Thunor (the Vikings' Thor), whom the Romans equated with Jove, associated with thunder and the stone hammer and a symbol for whom was the swastika, which possibly represented lightning; and Frija, the goddess of sexual love, also cognate with *freo,* as in *freond,* or "friend." The first four deities are memorialized in the days of the week: Tuesday, Wednesday, Thursday, and Friday. Eostre, a goddess of the dawn, according to Bede, gave her name to Easter. Not all deities remained potent. Nerthus, the great earth mother and a fertility goddess singled out by Tacitus, left no discernable mark, although there are many references in spells and Christian texts to what were clearly old fertility rites.

The persistence of belief in the old gods is often revealed in disapproving testimony of the church. Bishop Ælfric, writing as late as the late tenth century, for example, decries the manner in which his Christian flock still celebrates the new year: "Now foolish men

The ancient motif of broken crosses, also known as swastikas, decorates this urn from the fifth or sixth century from North Elmham, Norfolk.

OPPOSITE: Superstition and traditional knowledge played a large role in the Saxon psyche. This page from the *Old English Herbals* depicts parsley, cabbage, and a snake.

FOLLOWING PAGES: The Bewcastle Cross bears runic inscriptions from the Anglo-Saxon period.

THE PAGAN CALENDAR

We know little of Anglo-Saxon paganism but, oddly, relics of it survive in the calendar. Some of the days of the week are named after Germanic gods: Tuesday (Tiw's Day), Wednesday (Woden's Day), Thursday (Thunor's Day), Friday (Frija's Day). The nature of these gods has been forgotten over the centuries, but accounts recorded much later in Iceland provide an idea of them. Bede, who had an interest in the calendar, tells us the names of some of the pagan festivals: the feasts of the goddesses Hreda and Eostre took place in March (Hredmonath) and April (Eosturmonath, which gives us the name for Easter). This spring festival followed a period of fasting and culminated in the rebirth of vegetation and hope.

In February (Solmonath), as Bede tells us, cakes were offered to the gods. September was the Halegmonath, the holy month, and October to November was the Blodmonath, or blood month, when the Anglo-Saxons dedicated to the gods the animals to be culled in preparation for the fodder shortage of winter. Around midwinter came Modranect—mothers' night—an important period in the year when the days start to lengthen, a time of hope. It is no coincidence that this was the time chosen to celebrate the birth of Christ—the replacement of a pagan festival with a joyful Christian celebration. Anglo-Saxon paganism has left marks on the English landscape in the form of place-names. In Staffordshire, where the hoard was found, Wednesbury and Wednesfield were both named after the god Woden, the ancient sky god, and just down the road from the find spot is Weeford, a name that comes from *weoh*, the Old English name for a pagan shrine. Finally, what is the meaning of the strange animals and birds on the objects in the hoard itself? It is highly unlikely that they represent art for art's sake; these creatures carried meanings that are now lost to us, but we can still sense something of their power and mystery. ∎

A nobleman hunting with a falcon, a man on horseback, ducks in a pond, and Libra, October's astrological sign, are depicted on this 11th-century calendar page.

practice manifold sorceries on this day, with great error, after heathen custom, against their Christianity, as if it may lengthen their life, or their health, when [thus] they provoke the Almighty Creator. Also many are taken with as great an error, when they order their lives by the moon, and their deeds according to days."

The most effective way to combat the old heathen ways was to allow them to meld with Christian practices, as in a previous age the Romans had redirected aspects of Celtic faith by combining local gods with the classical pantheon. Local saints and relics came to fulfill the roles of pagan shrines and amulets. Indeed, the farsighted Pope Gregory advised early missionaries in England to convert heathen places of worship into churches, "in order that the people may the more familiarly resort to the places to which they have been accustomed."

In a famous story that according to Bede had "come down to us as a tradition of our forefathers," Gregory had been at a marketplace in Rome where among "other merchandise he saw some boys put up for sale, with fair complexions, handsome faces, and lovely hair. On seeing them he asked, so it is said, from what region or land they had been brought. He was told that they came from the island of Britain, whose inhabitants were like that in appearance." On learning the inhabitants were also heathens, Gregory had sighed, "and asked for the name of the race. He was told that they were Angli. 'Good,' he said, 'they have the faces of angels, and such men should be fellow-heirs of the angels in heaven.' "

In 597, which, as Bede notes, was "about 150 years after the coming of the Angles to Britain," Gregory dispatched Augustine (not to be confused with St. Augustine, the fifth-century bishop of Hippo) and some 40 other men of God to Britain as missionaries. En route, the delegation, overwhelmed by sudden awareness of the enormity of their task, "began to contemplate returning home rather than going to a barbarous, fierce and unbelieving nation whose language they did not even understand." Encouraged by Gregory, however, they persevered and landed in Kent, which was ruled by King Æthelberht, whose Frankish wife, Bertha, was a practicing Christian. The meeting between missionary and monarch took place, at Æthelberht's insistence, outside rather than in a building, lest the newcomers practice magic, which could at least be dissipated in the open air. Although he was not immediately converted, Æthelberht allowed Augustine and his companions to stay and pursue their mission, and granted them a base in Canterbury.

Although the English were heathen, many Britons had practiced Christianity under Roman rule, and their faith was safeguarded in British strongholds such as Wales, Cumbria, Cornwall, and Devon, as well as in Ireland. Nor was the Christian religion entirely unknown to the heathen: Not only was the wife of the king of Kent a Christian, but the religion would have been encountered by English who ventured abroad, or who came in contact with continentals, or who heard stories from others, both at home and abroad. This familiarity, however tenuous, was undoubtedly useful to the missionaries, as was an often-receptive curiosity on the part of the heathens, at least as reported by the Christian chroniclers. The missionaries were quick to target the high and mighty. The bond between Germanic lord and retainer was such that if a lord converted, those under him would follow.

"Reception of Saint Augustine by Ethelbert," painted by Stephen Reid (1873-1948), shows the future Archbishop of Canterbury being received by King Æthelberht of Kent in 597.

The concept of Christ the Lord, to whom one pledged one's life in fealty, was also straightforward to the Germanic heathen.

Greatly aided by the zealousness of the monastic-based missionaries of the Celtic church in Ireland, Christianity spread steadily in the north of Britain, and although enduring setbacks, progressed, remarkably, without the necessity of making a single martyr. By the mid-eighth century, England was sending missionaries of its own into the world. Indeed, the greatest battle for the new church was not with the unconverted heathen, but was an internal struggle between the Celtic and Roman churches. This conflict had important political and geographical implications, as the south of England had mostly been converted by missionaries from Rome, while the north, and especially Northumbria, had been converted in large part by missionaries from Ireland, where Christianity had developed outside the scope of Roman rule. The ostensible issue, incredible as it will seem today, concerned differences of opinion regarding calculation of the date for Easter, a moveable feast. The issue was debated and decided in favor of Rome in 664, at the Council of Whitby, in North Yorkshire. Thereafter, great Celtic monasteries, such as Lindisfarne, which had served as powerful centers of missionary activity and learning, were placed under the control of abbots obedient to Rome. At stake had been not so much a dispute over Easter, as the central authority of the increasingly powerful Church of Rome. The resolution, in any case, forced the unification of the English Church.

Several critical factors contributed to the conversion of the Anglo-Saxons—the rewiring of an entire population's spiritual and even intellectual culture. The replacement of Germanic beliefs, such as charms, amulets, and herbal spells, with Christian counterparts, such as holy water and the symbol of the cross, ensured that local people retained a level of comfort with new practices. At higher

PILGRIMAGES

The tradition of pilgrimage and religious exile arose very early in the Celtic church. Not long after the fall of Rome, Irish Christian monks were already heading out on pilgrimages "in the wilderness," often seeking penitence and sanctuary on islands (sometimes founding monasteries, such as St. Columba at Iona off Scotland in 653), but also preaching salvation among the pagans. It was considered a penance to leave the safety of one's own people to wander in the unknown.

Once the Anglo-Saxons converted, they too began pilgrimages to see relics of the saints in Rome and elsewhere, and they even went as far as Jerusalem and the Holy Land. Monks and nuns were frequent travelers, but laymen and women also traveled (though women were discouraged). Many English kings also journeyed to Rome, including Kings Caedwalla and Ine of Wessex, who voyaged in 688 and 728, respectively, and both died there.

It could take 12 weeks to travel between the English Channel and Rome, and throughout the arduous journey, monasteries and cathedral towns across what are now France, Switzerland, and Italy welcomed pilgrims. Many of these were holy destinations, such as Tours, Limoges, Conques, and Lucca. "Hospitals" arose to serve the needs of penitent pilgrims as well as the local poor, and other businesses benefited from the passing pilgrim trade.

A number of English holy men made the journey multiple times, often obtaining illustrated manuscripts and saintly relics for their monasteries. St. Benedict Biscop, born to a noble Anglo-Saxon family around 628, made five pilgrimages to Rome, where he collected books and relics for the monasteries he founded in 674 and 682: Wearmouth and Jarrow (home to Bede). Without Benedict's great libraries, Bede would not have been the finest scholar of his time. St. Wilfred, Bishop of York and a friend of Charlemagne's, traveled to Rome three times. His advocacy of Roman practice at the synod of Whitby in 664 helped it to prevail in the English Church. ■

The Pilgrims' Passage at Hexham Abbey, through which pilgrims viewed relics of St. Andrew

political levels, however, a key fact, as scholar Karen Jolly has put it, was that "the predominant theme . . . is the perception of the conversion event as a spiritual battle"—in other words, warfare, which was something the Germanic heathen understood. Actual battles, and more particularly victorious battles, had figured dramatically in the history of Christianity. Constantine, the first Christian emperor of ancient Rome, famously had converted following his victory at Milvian Bridge, having been "directed in a dream to cause the heavenly sign [the Chi Rho, a symbol of Christ] to be delineated on the shields of his soldiers." A tradition in Britain tells of the "battle of Badon, in which Arthur car-

ried the cross of our Lord Jesus Christ on his shoulders for three days and three nights, and the Britons were the victors." And Bede relates the story of the Northumbrian king Oswald, who before the Battle of Heavenfield against the Welsh in 634, "set up the sign of the holy cross, and on bended knees, prayed God to send heavenly aid to His worshippers in their dire need," following which he and his men "gained the victory that their faith merited."

The Christian writers, who by default are the chroniclers of this era, have left many testimonies concerning Christian members of their flocks turning superstitiously to heathen rites; but the opposite surely happened too, namely that Christian objects were turned to heathen use in heathen hands. This survey of faiths began with the question of why damaged Christian objects were included with Germanic-style military equipment in the Staffordshire Hoard. One explanation is that the objects have no particular significance at all, and are simply part of the spoils that an opportunistic looter grabbed from treasure close at hand. But it is at least possible that their presence may have something to do with the reputation of Christian icons for potency in battle; in other words, the crosses were weapons of a sort, and along with swords and helmets, they were best neutralized by ritual burial in the ground.

CHAPTER FOUR

THE LANGUAGE
OF MIDDLE EARTH

THE LANGUAGE OF MIDDLE EARTH

OPPOSITE: Offering tanta-lizing clues about the power of the written word, a strip of bent metal discovered with the Staffordshire Hoard bears a biblical verse.

PREVIOUS PAGES: The coast of Iona, in the Inner Hebrides Islands between Ireland and West Scotland, where it is believed the Book of Kells was begun in the late seventh or early eighth century

Folded almost in half and originally set with a now lost stone, a slender strip of gold alloy was one of the very few nonmilitary objects in the Staffordshire Hoard. At just over seven inches long and a little over half an inch wide, the gold strip is inscribed with a snake head and bears in clumsy lettering on both faces a misspelled biblical quotation—*"surge d[omi]ne [et] disepentur inimici tui et fugent qui oderunt te a facie tua"* ("Rise up, O Lord, and may Thy enemies be scattered and those who hate Thee flee from Thy face"). Viewed against the finely wrought cloisonné and glittering cut garnets, it would seem to be one of the hoard's more modest pieces. Yet no single object in the hoard has attracted so much speculation and difference of opinion. Two small holes bored through the strip presumably allowed it to be attached to something else—suggestions range from a helmet to an ecclesiastical object—while the strip itself may have formed the arm of a cross. Finally, there is the question of what if anything can be gleaned from the choice of quotation.

"When he had lifted up the Ark Moses said, 'Arise, O Lord, and let Thy enemies be scattered, and let those who hate Him flee before Him'"; thus runs the text of Numbers 10:35, the direct source of the quotation. A very similar variant, however, is that of Psalm 67:2: *"exsurgat Deus et dissipentur inimici eius et fugiant qui oderunt eum a facie eius"* ("*Let* God arise, let *His* enemies be scattered, and let those who hate *Him* flee from before *Him,*" Psalm 68:1 in modern editions).

As a number of scholars were quick to point out, the psalm's version would be the better known, given that the psalms were chanted daily in the monasteries; significantly, while the verse from Numbers does not appear in any ecclesiastical writings before the year 900, that of the psalm is found in a number of surviving works of the early church. And these early writings indicate that the Numbers/Psalm verses had at least one interesting and suggestive function. In the *Life of Saint Anthony*, which was translated into Latin (from the Greek of its author, Athanasius) around A.D. 370, Anthony retreats to the desert wilderness, where he is tempted by demons. Here, he "chanted that psalm inwardly: Let God arise, and let His enemies be scattered, and let them that hate Him flee before His face," and the demons were dispersed. This story of Anthony from late Roman times influenced a later and specifically Anglo-Saxon saintly "life," the *Life of Saint Guthlac*, written around 740. The biography tells how Guthlac, also beset by demons, "sang the first verse of the sixty-seventh psalm as if prophetically, 'Let God arise,' etc.: when they had heard this, at the same moment, quicker than words, all the hosts of demons vanished like smoke from his presence." As Brandon Hawk, the scholar who drew attention to this use, points out, these biographies of saints, or hagiographies, "present the psalm as a charm for warding off evil and achieving victory over the saints' enemies." The modest slip of gold, then, may have served the same kind of ritual function that scholars speculate for the two crosses also found in the hoard.

It is, however, not only the substance of the quotation on the gold strip, but also the fact of the writing itself, and the use of Latin, that is of interest. The Latin language was one of the great political and cultural legacies of Imperial Rome; it was also the language of learning and most particularly of the Catholic Church. (Even today Latin is the official language of the Vatican.)

Other systems of writing had also been known in Britain. As Tacitus had noted, the Germanic tribes on the Continent also had a system of reading lots, or divining the will of the gods, by marking strips of wood with "certain signs." These "signs" may have been runes, the system of symbols widely used by the Germans, and thought to have been first brought by Angles to England. The earliest surviving continental examples are from the early second century, but the date and origin of the runic system is unknown; a source in the German/Danish borderlands seems likely, and individual symbols owe clear debts to the Latin alphabet. Famously, the runes were believed to have magical properties, as a story told by Bede makes evident: Mercians captured a Northumbrian nobleman and put him in chains. But as often as he was bound, the chains would become loosened and fall away, and at length his amazed captor asked him if he had any "magical Runes" that caused this. In Bede's story, the miraculous loosening of the fetters turns out to have been the result of prayer, but the incident highlights what was evidently a widely known superstition.

Runes seem to have been mostly inscribed on wood; indeed, the angular character of the symbols may derive from the fact that they had to be carved. Descriptions of their use suggest that the magic did not reside in the symbols themselves, but in the spells and charms they inscribed. Runes were written in manuscripts, stamped on funerary pots, incised on jewelry, and carved decoratively onto a whalebone casket. One use in particular is striking: There are surviving Anglo-Saxon examples of the Scandinavian practice of inscribing runes on weapons, and one of the two known English examples of the entire 28-symbol runic alphabet appears on a seax, or single-edged sword, dredged from the Thames.

Widespread though the knowledge of runes seems to have been, the official language of politics, of business, of the church, indeed of everything that ran a kingdom, as well as of learning and scholarship, was Latin. In England, the caretaker of the Latin tongue, and therefore of literacy and learning in general, was the church.

The memory of Lindisfarne cast a long shadow over Christianity in northern England. A page from the medieval text "On the Estate of Lindisfarne" in *History of the Church of Durham*. The manuscript also contains histories of the community and church of St. Cuthbert, who became bishop of Lindisfarne in 635.

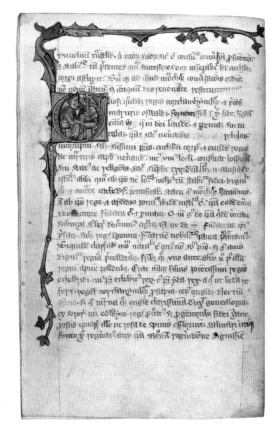

cholars generally hold two views of runes. One is that they were a mystery script used for ritual purposes. The other is that they had a more general use in administration and communication, and the fact that most of them are found in ritual contexts—on amulets, funerary urns, and weapons—is an accident of survival. The word *rune* (Old English *run*) and words like it have meanings like "council" and "consultation," which suggests that the alphabet was used in formal decision-making, but the same could be said of all writing. As well as having a sound value, each rune had a name: *d* was *daeg*, or "day," and *w* was *wynn*, or "joy." It appears that runes were developed for carving on wood, on which cutting straight lines is much easier than carving a curve. It also seems likely that the people who developed runes were familiar with the Latin alphabet. Runes continued to be used alongside the Roman alphabet throughout the Anglo-Saxon period. Runes were used on small objects, as well as on more than 70 sculptured monuments.

Runes surround an image of the Adoration of the Magi on the carved whalebone Franks Casket.

The silver wolf's head attached to this late-eighth-century knife mount from London was most likely meant to inspire bravery. The runes carved into the mount are presumably a magic charm offering protection.

Discovered in Greymoorhill, Carlisle, this eighth- to tenth-century gold ring is engraved with a runic inscription, three letters of which continue inside the hoop. The inscription is believed to have a magical connotation.

A delicate fifth-century repoussé gold bracteate pendant with a runic inscription and a depiction of Romulus and Remus.

The Thames River yielded this tenth-century iron seax, or knife, inscribed with two texts: One is a 28-letter runic alphabet; the other is a name in Old English.

OPPOSITE: A 1799 water-color depicts Alfred the Great as a child, kneeling by his mother, Queen Judith, as she recites the songs of the bards.

This was due not to any reverence for the humanities or education per se, but to the pragmatic need to have men who could read and give instruction in the Scriptures. In *A Colloquy*, Bishop Ælfric, who taught and wrote in the late tenth century, gives a vivid account of a dialogue between an instructor and his pupils:

Pupil: We children beg you, teacher, to show us how to speak Latin correctly, for we are ignorant, and speak inaccurately.
Teacher: What do you want to talk about?
Pupil: What do we care what we talk about, if only it be correctly spoken and useful, not trivial or base?

While the early English Church promoted the use of Latin as a necessary tool in its mission to propagate the Christian faith, the cultivation of the liberal arts—the great legacy of Greece and Rome—was the passionate and dedicated work of the Irish monasteries. Not only was the monastic scholarship of the highest order in Europe, but, remarkably, study of the sacred texts was combined with the works of secular writers such as Virgil, Horace, Ovid, Cicero, and Pliny.

In England, the church was keenly conscious of the seductive power of pagan poetry and stories, whether classical or, closer to home, Germanic. In what has been called "one of the most famous letters in Anglo-Saxon," written in 797, Alcuin, renowned as a teacher as well as a scholar of high learning and a minister of education of sorts to Charlemagne, scolds Bishop Higbald of the Lindisfarne monastery, where dreadful rumor had it that the brethren had been listening not to grave sermons of the fathers of the church, but to heathen song:

The words of God should be read at the monks' feasts. There the reader should be heard not a harpist, the discourses of the Fathers not the songs of the heathens. What has Ingeld to do with Christ? [Ingeld is a warrior who appears in both Scandinavian and Old English saga, including the poem Beowulf.] The house is narrow, it cannot contain both. The king of the heavens will have nothing to do with heathen and damned so-called kings. For the Eternal King rules in the heavens, the lost heathen repines in hell. The voices of readers should be heard in your houses, not the cackling of the crowd in the street.

THE POWER OF WRITING

Among the Staffordshire Hoard's many notable objects, one of the most intriguing is a strip of metal bearing a biblical inscription, powerful words of great meaning to the people who commissioned them. Many existing inscriptions from Anglo-Saxon England show how much importance was attached to the written word. Prior to the advent of Christianity in England, writing took the form of Germanic runes, used by the Anglo-Saxons for short, often obscure, inscriptions on such things as brooches and pots. Most likely created by people familiar with the Roman alphabet, runes were used in northern Europe around the fourth century A.D. The letters were made up of short, straight lines, ideal for cutting onto wood, stone, or other hard materials. As Christianity is a religion of the book with great emphasis on the written word, St. Augustine's proselytizing mission to Britain in A.D. 597 promoted the Roman alphabet. Within a few years of his arrival, the Anglo-Saxons were producing their own books, their designs fusing with those of their Irish neighbors to give us the wonders of insular art, represented by the Book of Durrow, the Lindisfarne Gospels, and the Book of Chad.

People continued using runes long after the introduction of the Roman alphabet. The eighth-century stone cross from Ruthwell, Dumfriesshire, bears, in runes, part of the great Anglo-Saxon poem "The Dream of the Rood." An eighth-century seax, or single-edged sword, found in the River Thames bears, on one of its sides, a *futhorc*, or runic alphabet, known from its opening letters: F – U – Th – O – R – C. Its owner may have believed that these letters represented the basis of all written texts, including the Bible. The inscription on a tenth-century seax from Sittingbourne is more down-to-earth; on one side, written in Old English using Roman letters, are the words, "Sigebereht owns me." On the other side are the words "Biorthelme made me," an early example of product branding. ∎

Fulda Manuscript: Accompanied by Alcuin of York, Rabanus Maurus, the Benedictine monk and theologian, presents his work to Archbishop Otgar of Mainz.

One imagines the crestfallen faces of the rebuked monks who had enjoyed these recitals of heroic tales of derring-do in the remote quiet of their sanctuaries.

The "cackling" crowd obviously did not speak, let alone read, Latin. Their language was what we refer to today as Old English, or Anglo-Saxon, their Germanic tongue. The fact that the language of the church, as well as the language of education, was conducted in a tongue most of the populace could not understand would not necessarily have been problematic to the masses. After all, both Celtic and Germanic cultures, like many others, had long, venerated traditions of sacral languages, as preserved in song and verse. But one person who did find this disjunction undesirable was King Alfred—Alfred the Great—who, among his many accomplishments, was an educational reformer and a pioneering translator of Latin works. A biography of Alfred, written shortly after 893, describes the formative childhood of this Christian king and his early attraction to the stories of his own people:

This elegant ninth century silver brooch, made about the time of the Viking conquest, cleverly shows the five senses: Sight appears in the center surrounded by smell, touch, hearing, and taste.

His noble birth and noble nature implanted in him from his cradle a love of wisdom above all things, even amid all the occupations of this present life; but—with shame be it spoken!—by the unworthy neglect of his parents he remained illiterate till he was twelve years old or more, though by night and day he was an attentive listener to the Saxon poems which he often heard being recited.

In a well-known letter written to Bishop Wærferth in the late ninth century, Alfred himself describes how he came to his self-imposed task: "When I remembered how the knowledge of Latin had formerly decayed throughout England, and yet many could read English writing, I began, among other various and manifold troubles of this kingdom, to translate into English the book which is called in Latin *Pastoralis*, and in English *Shepherd's Book* sometimes word by word, and sometimes according to the sense."

FOLLOWING PAGE: A page from a copy of the Venerable Bede's "Life of St. Cuthbert" illustrated manuscript depicts a Benedictine monk kissing the feet of St. Cuthbert, who is vested as a bishop.

Lost Gold of the Dark Ages

Alfred's systematic educational reform saw the cultivation of instruction in reading and writing the English language. Fittingly, his biography, quoted above, is the first secular biography in English. Literary English had been used before this, in both poetry and prose, but not widely. According to tradition, the first English Christian poem was composed by Caedmon, a brother in the monastery at Whitby, who, according to Bede, "did not learn the art of poetry from men nor through a man but he received the gift of song freely by the grace of God." Although his work was renowned in his lifetime, only one of his poems, "Caedmon's Hymn," has survived:

> *Now shall we praise   the Prince of heaven,*
> *The might of the Maker   and his manifold thought,*
> *The work of the Father: of what wonders he wrought*
> *The Lord everlasting,   when he laid out the worlds.*
> *He first raised up   for the race of men*
> *The heaven as a roof,   the holy Ruler.*
> *Then the world below,   the Ward of mankind,*
> *As a home for man,   the Almighty Lord.*

The attested wide popularity of this modest work—17 copies of it survive—undoubtedly lay not only in its charm and freshness but also, as one scholar speculated, in the fact that Caedmon was the first to apply "Germanic heroic poetic discipline of vocabulary, style and general technique to Christian story and Christian edification." The quotation above is itself a translation, from Old English into modern English; to appreciate its Germanic features, such as the alliteration and emphatic caesura, or pause, within each verse, the poem must be read in the original:

> *Nu scylun hergan   hefaenricaes uard,*
> *metudæs maecti   end his modgidanc,*
> *uerc uuldurfadur   sue he uundra gihuaes,*
> *eci dryctin   or astelidæ.*
> *He areist scop   aelda barnum*
> *heben til hrofe,   haleg scepen;*

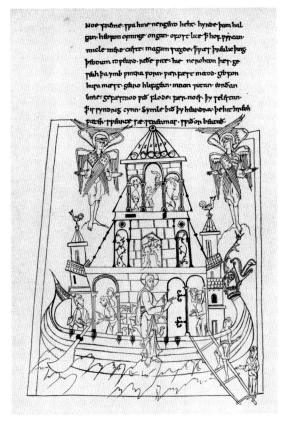

The Anglo-Saxons saw Christianity in terms of their own world. In this tenth-century manuscript Noah's ark takes the form of a Viking ship.

FOLLOWING PAGES: The 16th-century ruins of Lindisfarne Castle loom over the Holy Island located on England's northeastern coast. Home to a monastery founded by St. Aidan around 635, this is where the illuminated Lindisfarne Gospels were produced.

LOST GOLD OF THE DARK AGES

tha middungeard	moncynnæs uard,
eci dryctin,	æfter tiadæ,
firum foldu	frea allmectig.

This short poem reveals its Germanic character not only in its poetic technique but also in its vocabulary. Caedmon's choice of word—*middungeard,* or "Middle Earth"—for the place under God's heaven inhabited by man, is an echo of the old Nordic cosmological belief in nine worlds connected by a rainbow.

Like the first English poem, the first surviving English prose is a Christian work. The anonymous *Life of St. Cuthbert,* generally dated between 698 to 705, or less than 20 years after the saint's death, is believed to have been written by a monk of Lindisfarne Abbey, where Cuthbert had been bishop. In his preface to his great *Ecclesiastical History,* Bede refers to this work as a source for his own—"accepting the story I read in simple faith," but also making it his business "to add with care what I was able to learn myself." Bede himself later wrote two lives of this popular saint, one in prose and one in verse.

Despite their Christian subject matter, the Early English works resonate with the old heroic songs and sagas; as Alcuin's indignant letter revealed, these were enjoyed and perpetuated within monastic walls, the very centers of English learning. Their popularity can be attributed in great part to the fact that men and women from the aristocracy accounted for so large and influential a part of the monastic populations—it is estimated that between the seventh and early eighth centuries, some 30 kings and queens entered monasteries, along with countless other men and women of noble birth, warriors, and court retainers. Heroic tales of warriors winning glory were the fare these monks of the nobility had learned as children, just as King Alfred had listened to the Saxon poems in his boyhood. In the many hagiographic works of this period, the saint becomes the "hero of God," or "the warrior of the Lord," performing prodigies of saintly deeds. When he was a boy, St. Guthlac was "in his father's halls, trained in the noble traditions of his ancestors," and later, "when his youthful strength had grown greater . . . he called to mind the mighty deeds of heroes of old and, like one roused from slumber he put aside his former disposition, gathered about him troops of followers, and took to a life of war."

Along with this reverberation of Nordic heroic lore, Early English literature, and poetry in particular is infused with a melancholy yearning often attributed to the even older Celtic traditions still potent in the Irish monasteries, where so many churchmen of England had trained, especially in the late seventh century. Whether from a Celtic sense of loss, as is supposed, or a Germanic yearning for a now distant

Above: St. Matthew, as depicted in the Lindisfarne Gospels
Below: Illuminated page from the beginning of St. Matthew's Gospel

OPPOSITE: Introductory carpet page from St. Matthew's Gospel, Lindisfarne Gospels.

King and Church were closely associated in Anglo-Saxon England. Here Cnut, the Viking king who conquered England in 1016, accompanied by his wife Aelfgifu, presents a jewelled cross to the Minster at Winchester.

homeland, the melancholy is unmistakable, and often expressed in terms of exile: *The Wanderer, The Seafarer, Wulf and Eadwacer, The Wife's Lament*—in all these poems, the speaker bares his or her soul to pour out a story of loss and grief. Says the forsaken heroine of *The Wife's Lament*,

LOST GOLD OF THE DARK AGES

LIFE IN A MONASTERY

The life of a medieval monk, following St. Benedict's regulations of A.D. 529, was one of chastity, poverty, and extreme obedience. Monks spoke no word but prayer, ate tasteless foods, and lived a rigorous daily life enclosed in walls. Prayers began at two in the morning and ended at sunset, with services every three hours between. Otherwise, monks were either at hard physical work or copying the words of religious texts, if not writing works of their own. Their main meal, lunch, consisted of bland fare such as poached fish or gruel. They were not permitted to leave the compound without permission of the abbot, and they could not own property or send or receive letters from home.

What was the appeal of such an existence?

Life in a monastery was strict and hard, but in a troubled and transient world everyone's prime concern was to save his soul from hell. Monks and nuns were drawn almost exclusively from the aristocracy, although we do see a few exceptions such as the poet Caedmon. Kings like Sigeberht and Aethelred of Mercia retired to monasteries, which played a vital role in protecting a kingdom. The Viking raids were seen as God's punishment. In response, Alfred sought to reform the church and improve the level of religious training so that God would protect his people. An odd feature of Anglo-Saxon monasteries was the existence of double houses, which contained both monks and nuns, living parallel but separate lives under the control of an abbess. Not all monasteries were equally valued; in his letter to Egberht of York, Bede criticizes the low standards of some, which were, in effect, aristocratic households disguised as monasteries to avoid taxes.

Monasteries became the centers of education and progressive thinking. Some of them were very rich, with massive landholdings and noted craftsmen and -women. Many failed to survive the Viking onslaught and had to be refounded, sometimes after the Norman Conquest. ∎

Monks urge St. Cuthbert to accept the bishopric of Lindisfarne in 635 in this illustration from Bede's *Life of St. Cuthbert*.

LOST GOLD OF THE DARK AGES

I am anxious with longing.
Dim are the dales,   dark the hills tower,
Bleak the tribe-dwellings,   with briars entangled,
Unblessed abodes.   Here bitterly I have suffered
The faring of my lord afar.   Friends there are on earth
Living in love,   in lasting bliss,
While, wakeful at dawn,   I wander alone
Under the oak-tree   the earth-cave near.

Sometimes this melancholy nostalgia extends beyond the speaker's own circumstances to the tragic panorama of bygone lives and times: "I cannot think why in the world / my mind does not darken when I brood on the fate / of brave warriors," says the speaker of *The Wanderer;* "how they have suddenly / had to leave the mead-hall, the bold followers. / So this world dwindles day by day, / and passes away."

This melancholy, the awareness of the passing of an age, also infuses the heroic epic *Beowulf,* the masterpiece of Anglo-Saxon, or Old English, literature—and a work that represents the fusion of traditions and sensibilities that makes the Early English literary tradition so extraordinary. In story line, *Beowulf* is pure Nordic saga, a tale of the Geat, or Swedish, warrior Beowulf's heroic feats, which culminate in the slaying of the swamp monster Grendel, of "Cain's clan," and of his mother. In the second part of the poem, the aged Beowulf is king of the Geats and confronts a dragon guarding a hoard of gold. Beowulf, praised for such virtues as truthfulness and devotion to justice, slays the dragon and, dying from his wounds, gives thanks to "the everlasting Lord of All, / to the King of Glory." Thus, while the hero is Germanic, the misty bog atmosphere both Celtic and Nordic, the influence of the Roman *Aeneid* palpable, the Anglo-Saxon epic is shot through with Christian sensibilities.

King Alfred's reformation of England's educational system was given urgency by the damage inflicted on monastic centers by the Viking raids that mauled England from the end of the eighth century onward, exacerbating what had been a general decline in scholarship. The monasteries, with their well-known and undefended treasures, had been particular targets: Lindisfarne, for example, was sacked on June 8, 793. As part of his reform, Alfred invited distinguished scholars from the Continent to advise and educate the future English educators whose own standards of learning had slipped. Along with the many books that filled the great libraries before the catastrophic Viking raids, Alfred recalled, "there was also a great multitude of God's

OPPOSITE: Suggesting some of the demonic themes in the text of *Beowulf,* the 11th-century manuscript "Wonders of the East" features a disturbing portrait of a red-eyed demon reaching from the depths of hell in an effort to claim another soul.

FOLLOWING PAGES: The 118 surviving folios (double pages) of the Gospels of St. Chad, housed in the library at Lichfield Cathedral in Staffordshire, date from 730 and contain some of the earliest examples of written Welsh.

In addition to defending the Anglo-Saxon kingdoms of southern England against Vikings, Alfred the Great, who ruled from 871 to 899, famously encouraged the use of English over Latin in education.

servants, but they had very little knowledge of the books, for they could not understand anything of them, because they were not written in their own language." It was Alfred's belief that the Vikings were God's way of punishing his people for their neglect of his word. While the cultivation of Latin in the church was encouraged, Alfred set forth a visionary new program:

BEOWULF

Beowulf is an epic story of a great hero who defeats fearsome foes and eventually dies in battle against the last of them. The 3,182-line poem takes us back to another world, similar to the world that produced the Staffordshire Hoard. Although the date of the poem's composition has been much debated, it was likely written down in the later eighth or early ninth century. While clearly Anglo-Saxon, it is set in Scandinavia and, despite Christian elements, reflects a pagan world, perhaps of the sixth century.

Hrothgar, king of the Danes, having gained glory and reputation in battle, builds Heorot, a magnificent mead hall. The sounds of happiness and celebration attract the attention of Grendel, a monster "descended from Cain," who each night raids the hall, killing and kidnapping men to his den in the fens. Beowulf, a Geat from what is now southern Sweden, hears of this horror and, with his chosen companions, sails to Denmark to destroy the monster. Weaponless, he waits for Grendel, who, on arriving, kills and eats a man. Beowulf is to be next. As he catches Grendel in his iron grip, warriors rush to his aid. The monster is proof against their swords but not against Beowulf's strength: Beowulf tears Grendel's arm from his shoulder. Dying, the fiend flees back to his den. The celebration of this deliverance is cut short by the arrival of Grendel's mother, seeking vengeance for her son. Called on to remove the new menace, Beowulf dives deep into a pool

and kills her. He then returns to the Geats and is crowned king. He rules for 50 years until someone steals a golden cup from a hoard guarded by a dragon. Enraged, the dragon starts to burn the Geats' land, and the aged Beowulf once more is called to action. In the ensuing battle, both he and the dragon die.

What does this remarkable poem tell us about the Staffordshire Hoard? It is full of references to the objects the hoard comprises—swords, spears, helmets, and treasure—and, not surprisingly, shows their great importance to Anglo-Saxon aristocrats. It also tells of loyalty, the relationship between a warrior and his lord, and the rewards given and promises made in the mead hall. Most important, *Beowulf* tells of deposits of treasure guarded from an older age. ■

A page from the earliest known manuscript of *Beowulf*, dating to ca 1000

The savage 793 destruction of Lindisfarne by Norse raiders is recorded in the Lindisfarne Stone, which was likely erected to commemorate the dead. The other side of the stone bears a scene from the Day of Judgment.

OPPOSITE: Christ's entry into Jerusalem is pictured on this page from The Benedictional of St. Aethelwold, a masterpiece of Anglo-Saxon book painting. The miniature was made for Aethelwold, Bishop of Winchester from 963 to 984 and an important figure in the late tenth-century monastic revival.

Therefore it seems better to me . . . for us also to translate some books which are most needful for all men to know into the language which we can all understand, and for you to do as we very easily can if we have tranquility enough, that is, that all the youth now in England of free men, who are rich enough to be able to devote themselves to it, be set to learn as long as they are not fit for any other occupation, until they are able to read English writing well: and let those be afterwards taught more in the Latin language who are to continue in learning, and be promoted to higher rank.

Alfred's initiative was the beginning of a long process of transformation, but by the end of the ninth century English was beginning to replace Latin as the language of law and business and was used for official documents including wills and charters. This widespread use of the vernacular in England and Ireland was, before the 12th century, unique in Europe.

According to Caesar, as we've seen, the Druids did not commit their traditions and lore to writing "since it generally occurs to most men, that, in their dependence on writing, they relax their diligence in learning thoroughly, and their employment of the memory." As the Druids had feared, the spread of literacy and books did indeed erode those traditions that had been born and shaped by memory, the many orally transmitted songs and poems that had celebrated and preserved the old heroic values—songs as old as those heard by Tacitus centuries ago, before Germanic tribes had crossed the sea to Britain. Few of these Germanic poems survive, the Christian monks and monastic-based scholars being, perhaps understandably, uninterested in the recording of heathen verse.

On the other hand, the potency of the written word had been manifested even in resolutely oral cultures—how else to account for the Druidic use of "symbols" to divine the will of god or fate, or the runic inscriptions determinedly etched on burial goods and weapons, and, possibly, on crosses? *"[S]urge d[omi]ne [et] dispentur inimici tui et fugent qui oderunt te a facie tua"*—"Rise up, O Lord, and may Thy enemies be scattered and those who hate Thee flee from Thy face": Do the belligerent words on the strip of gold found in the Staffordshire Hoard, then, represent some early faith in the literal magic of the written word?

CHAPTER FIVE

GOLD IN THE GROUND

*"rummage the hoard ... be as quick as you can
so that I may see/the age-old store of gold, and
examine/all the priceless shimmering stones"*

— BEOWULF

GOLD IN THE GROUND

oins, pottery, burials, buried treasure, hoards: England's soil is dense with history. In A.D. 418, according to the *Anglo-Saxon Chronicle*, even after the Roman army had officially left England, "the Romans collected all the hoards of gold that were in Britain; and some they hid in the earth, so that no man afterwards might find them, and some they carried with them into Gaul." A hoard can take many forms; hoards of late Roman coin and plate in Scotland and Ireland have been found hacked up—the loot, as it seems, of Pictish or Scottish or other barbarian raids. The Hoxne Treasure, found in Suffolk and dating from the late fourth century, with its 16,000 coins of gold and silver, plate, and jewelry, is one of the largest such finds from anywhere in the Roman Empire. The Mildenhall Treasure, also from Suffolk and the late fourth century, is a 27-piece silver dinner service of the highest workmanship. The Thetford Hoard, found in Norfolk, consists of late Roman plate and jewelry. The fifth-century Patching Hoard holds gold and silver coinage and jewelry from East Sussex.

Hoards are found in all eras. The Langton Matravers Hoard and Ambleside Hoard date from the Bronze Age. The Westerham Hoard is Iron Age, the Frome Hoard Roman. The Vale of York Hoard, found as recently as 2007 in North Yorkshire, was a ninth-century Viking hoard of broken jewelry, coins, and silver ingots. On the upper floor of the British Museum, one can look down a line of display cases spanning over a thousand years of hoards found in Britain.

OPPOSITE: England's soil has borne other archaeological treasures over the centuries. The Didcot Hoard, pictured here, may have been a gift from Emperor Marcus Aurelius to his senior officials in the first or second century.

PREVIOUS PAGES: Fred Johnson is pictured in the field on his farm where the Staffordshire Hoard was discovered after lying buried for 1,300 years in what was then the Anglo-Saxon kingdom of Mercia.

This magnificent fourth-century silver vessel is known as the Oceanus Dish and is part of another hoard, the Mildenhall Treasure. Its imagery alludes to the worship and mythology of Bacchus on land and sea.

Treasure hoards haunt the literature as well as fill the ground. Within the epic *Beowulf*, Sigemund kills a dragon guarding a treasure hoard "with dazzling spoils." At the conclusion of the epic, the aged Beowulf himself battles a dragon guarding another hoard of treasure that was laid in the earth in a bygone age. Mortally wounded by the dragon, Beowulf urges his loyal young companion, Wiglaf, to "rummage the hoard . . . be as quick as you can so that I may see/the age-old store of gold, and examine/all the priceless shimmering stones."

And treasure hoards tantalize the imagination. Today, droves of treasure seekers equipped with sophisticated metal-detecting equipment tramp the fields every year, seeking and sometimes finding relics of Britain's many bygone ages—Iron Age, Roman, Anglo-Saxon, Viking, Norman, medieval. And on the morning of July 5, 2009, veteran metal detector operator Terry Herbert came upon a trove of Anglo-Saxon objects buried near the village of Hammerwich, Staffordshire, in farmer Fred Johnson's field.

This field, which the farmer most recently had used to grow turnips and brussels sprouts as well as to graze horses and cattle, was in Anglo-Saxon times an unpopulated area of woodlands and coarse heath—the kind of remote area in which wary travelers kept a lookout for highwaymen as late as the mid-17th century. Two folk groups, or tribes, shared the region—the Pencersaete and Tomsaete, from the valleys of the Rivers Penk and Tame respectively. Tame, like the Thames, reflects an old Celtic name meaning the "dark" or "slow-flowing" water. It is thought the land was used not for habitation, but for seasonal grazing by people from outlying estates, which later records indicate included estates at Wednesbury and Wolverhampton—good Germanic names.

Cutting through this region was Watling Street, one of the major arteries of transportation built and left by the Romans, and still in use in Anglo-Saxon times (and, in many parts of England, still in use today). The road ran through the former Roman town of Letocetum (later Wall), whose ruins would also probably have been visible, some two and half miles to the east of where the hoard was buried. Letocetum derives from Old Welsh/Celtic *Lwytgoed*, "the gray wood or forest," as similarly the nearby town Lichfield is "the *feld*—open country, or common pasture—beside the gray wood." The preponderance of nearby place-names (some surviving today, some preserved in old charters) with the Old English *leah*—"open woodland"—such as Wyrley and Oggeleye also evokes the

Veteran metal detector hobbyist Terry Herbert holds the equipment that led him to the first objects from the Staffordshire Hoard in 2009.

FOLLOWING PAGES: Autumn mist over Hathersage, Derbyshire, part of the ancient kingdom of Mercia

vanished landscape. In the mid-to-late seventh century, the Roman road and ruins were most likely the only human-made elements in this somewhat forbidding heath fringed by gray-green forest when, one day or night, some unknown party stepped off the road onto the rise of a small hill and buried a stash of garnet-studded treasure in the ground.

In the wider landscape, the site of the hoard sat squarely in the heart of Mercia, one of the most important of the seven kingdoms into which Anglo-Saxon–era England was, in a rough-and-tumble way, divided. Only some seven miles to the northeast, Tamworth, a royal estate in the seventh century, was to become the capital of Mercia; Lichfield, about three miles to the north, was made the episcopal see of Mercia in 669. The region was Anglian, as opposed to Saxon or Frisian or another Germanic tribe's, and the name Mercia refers to a "march" or "boundary"—in other words, a border country, although whether the border in question was among geographically dispersed Angles, or between Angles and the Welsh to the west, is unclear.

Frustratingly little is known about this powerful and strategic kingdom in the formative seventh century, and the little that is known mostly comes from the Northumbrian Bede. Among other reasons, the discovery of the Staffordshire Hoard was exciting for being, in the words of one historian, "something tangible from . . . mid- to late-seventh-century Mercia." The kingdom emerged in the region of the Upper Trent on the frontier between Welsh and Anglo-Saxon territory. Some scholars believe the origins of the kingdom lie with a group of Angles who moved inland up the Humber Estuary in the fifth century and established themselves in the Trent Valley, in the region of the hoard. Here, with their Viking-like prowess as raiders and warriors as well as settlers, they gained ascendency over small groups. By the seventh century they were no longer a mixed collection of different peoples, but Mercians, inhabiting an identifiable kingdom, albeit one whose borders

The Kingdom of Mercia

The English Midlands, where the Staffordshire Hoard was discovered, sit squarely in the Anglo-Saxon kingdom of Mercia. Some three miles north of the find is Lichfield, the Mercians' ecclesiastic center, and just seven miles to the east lies Tamworth, a major royal site. Mercia's name comes from the Old English word *mierce*, which means "boundary," but it is unclear who inhabited the other side. Though we assume it was the Welsh, it could also have referred to the Anglo-Saxons to the north, with whom the Mercians fought bitterly. Or perhaps the term described people who lived to the west of the main area of Anglian settlement in eastern England. Some believe it was the Mercians who inspired the Riders of the Mark, the mounted soldiers of the land of Rohan (also called Riddermark or the Mark), in J. R. R. Tolkien's *Lord of the Rings*.

The hoard must have been gathered during the seventh century, when Mercia was a rising power under Kings Penda (ca 632–655) and Wulfhere (658–674). In the eighth century Mercian domination extended over much of England, under Kings Æthelbald (716–757) and Offa (757–796), whose power reached as far south as London, east to the kingdoms of East Anglia and Essex, and as far north as the Humber. A stupendous monument—the massive, 64-mile long earthwork known as Offa's Dyke—marked the boundary with the Welsh. Greater Mercia came apart during the ninth century, which saw the rise of the Kingdom of Wessex. In A.D. 879 the Vikings took over large areas of Mercia, and it became part of the Danelaw, where Danish law prevailed. The last ruler of Mercia, King Alfred's daughter, Aethelflaed, the Lady of the Mercians, took control after the death of her husband, Aethelred. Following Aethelflaed's own death in A.D. 918, King Edward of Wessex removed Aethelflaed's daughter, Aelfwynn, and ruled Mercia. The kingdom was amalgamated with Wessex and disappeared as England came into existence. ■

Offa holds a model of St. Albans Abbey, which he founded ca 793.

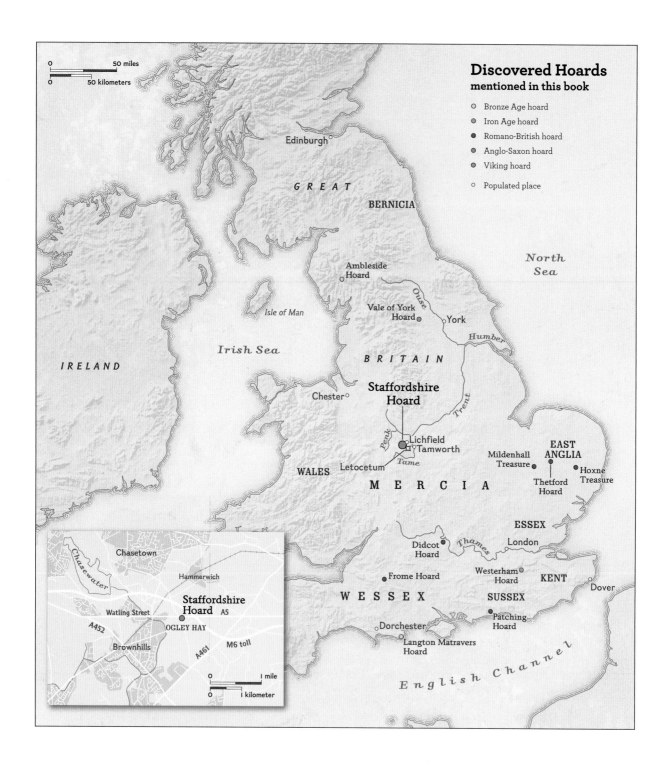

changed with each battle. According to Bede, the kingdom contained some 12,000 hides—a hide being the amount of land necessary to sustain a household—and was divided into northern and southern regions by the River Trent.

It is clear that the central forces behind Mercia's expansion were the movements and character of King Penda, who, according to Bede, was "a most energetic member of the royal house of Mercia." Penda was made king in 632 but seems to have won a name for himself as a battle lord of the old Germanic school well before this time. In genealogy, Penda and his dynastic line claimed to be descended from the god Woden and, perhaps more politically relevant, the rulers who held sway over the continental Anglians before the migration to England. The most formidable king of his generation, Penda battled fellow Anglians to the north and east, Saxons to the south, and the British in Wales to the west, and his victories on these many fronts made Mercia powerful. Mercia's run of good fortune had a setback with Penda's defeat and death in 655, in a landmark battle against the king of Bernicia to the north. We shall return later to this campaign and its possible implications for the Staffordshire Hoard.

"Gold in the ground—the epic *Beowulf* is shot through with descriptions of gold. The hero Scyld is reverently buried with "a gold standard up/high above his head"; King Finn must honor the Danes with "the wrought-gold rings . . . to keep morale in the beer-hall high"; a funeral pyre is heaped "with boar-shaped helmets forged in gold"; Finn's halls are sacked, and his "gold collars and gemstones—swept off to the ship"; and Beowulf is presented with "a gold-chased heirloom . . . the best example/of a gem-studded sword in the Geat treasury." In *Beowulf* a king is *goldwine gumena*, the gold friend of warriors, or a *gold-gyfa*, a *beag-gyfa*—a giver of gold, a giver of rings.

Gold is associated with divinity as well as nobility. Germanic myths tell of the gods' great hall of gold, and as Christian churches and monasteries gained wealth they acquired golden sacral objects; one of the Staffordshire Hoard's two golden crosses, it will be recalled, is thought to have been an altar or a processional cross. From at least Roman times, gold was held to have magic properties and was used

Another treasure of the kingdom of Mercia, this carving of an angel, which dates to about 800, was discovered in 2003 during the excavation of the Lichfield Cathedral.

OPPOSITE: The mid- to late seventh century, when archaeologists believe the Staffordshire Hoard was deposited, was a time of great tumult; here, Penda of Mercia is slain by King Oswiu's army in 655.

in protective amulets; and ancient magical recipes specify that love charms and curses alike be written on tablets of gold. Gold appears in ritual deposits made in lakes and bogs and the earth, including deposits of objects that have been deliberately broken and rendered useless, like those of the Staffordshire Hoard.

And gold accounts for nearly 75 percent of the metal composition of the Staffordshire Hoard itself, whose delicate individual golden pieces cumulatively amount to over 11 pounds. For the most part, the gold used by Anglo-Saxons had been recycled. Local gold and silver mines, situated in the British Celtic–controlled north and west, were off-limits, and available gold mostly came from Rome, whose imperial currency had been based on the *solidus*, or solid gold coin. Imperial gold had come to the Germanic tribes first as military pay, then, following the sack of Rome, as plunder, while the surviving eastern empire, Byzantium, paid the barbarians gold to keep away. Additional gold entered England in the form of diplomatic gifts, a key component of the Germanic nobility's gift-giving culture.

By the time of the Staffordshire Hoard, however, the availability of gold in England was dwindling. Pure gold had become scarcer and alloys of silver more prevalent, along with silver jewelry and coinage. International trade in garnets had also shifted. Germanic jewelers and craftsmen had introduced a cloisonné technique to Europe, using slices of polished garnets and other gemstones, that were either imported raw, or possibly already cut into sheets as fine as 1 millimeter (0.04 inch) thick. Historically, garnets mostly originated in India and were brought to Europe via the Silk Road. In the late sixth century, however, this source dried up, possibly due to disruption in the east caused by the Persian invasion of southern Arabia. From this time, Bohemia and Portugal became the most common suppliers, although of inferior stones. The preciousness, and possible scarceness, of garnets is suggested by an interesting feature discovered in the process of cleaning objects of the hoard; two of the duller garnets of item K674, a striking gold and garnet pommel cap of a sword, turned out on close inspection to be in fact red glass.

Details of materials and technique are of particular interest to the archaeologists

and historians interpreting the Staffordshire Hoard, for these are the tools they must work with in the all-important task of establishing the hoard's date. The land in which the hoard had lain for 13 centuries became a working field—a field, in other words, that was not only grazed, but also plowed and generally disturbed. Plowing and erosion churned the hoard into the upper layers of the earth, and so when Terry Herbert discovered the objects, they were lying near the surface. The archaeological context for the hoard, then, had long been destroyed, and in order to date the finds archaeologists must rely on features of the objects themselves—the materials used, the techniques of composition, and the artistic style.

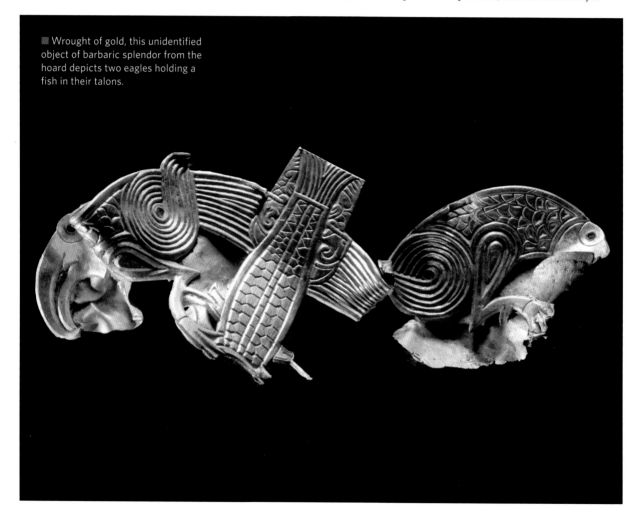

Wrought of gold, this unidentified object of barbaric splendor from the hoard depicts two eagles holding a fish in their talons.

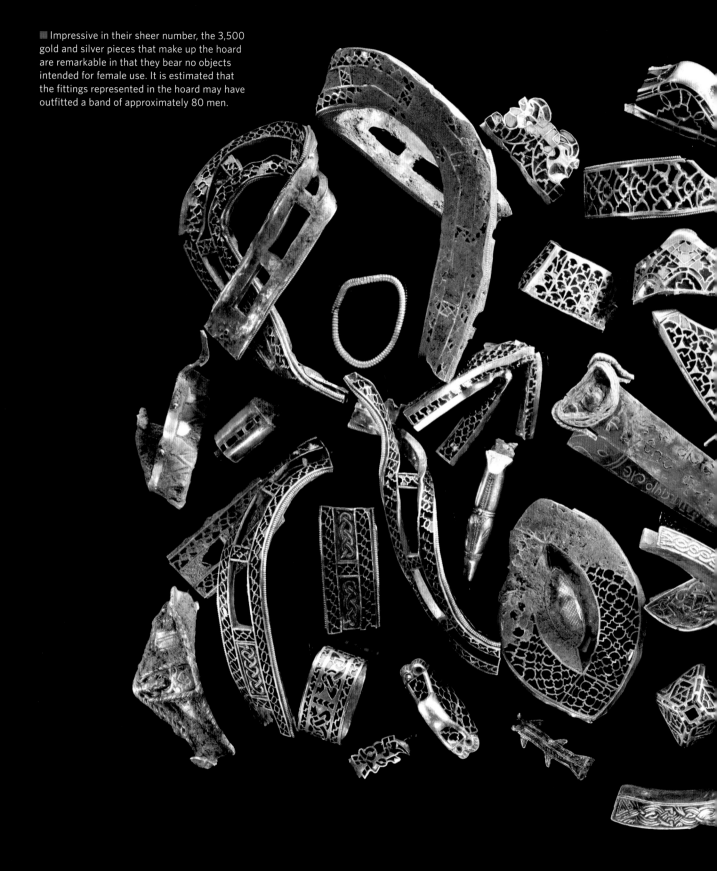

Impressive in their sheer number, the 3,500 gold and silver pieces that make up the hoard are remarkable in that they bear no objects intended for female use. It is estimated that the fittings represented in the hoard may have outfitted a band of approximately 80 men.

The "step" pattern of the seventh-century Anglo-Saxon Kingston Down Brooch recalls the center of the St. Mark carpet page in the Lindisfarne Gospels, a collection of illuminated manuscripts produced in Lindisfarne in Northumbria around 715.

"There is nothing that looks in any way Celtic," according to Kevin Leahy, a leading Anglo-Saxon authority and the first person to catalog the hoard. "It is wholly Germanic." Art historians classify Germanic art of this early "conversion" period on the basis of its iconography, or the kind of pictures and images the craftsman has chosen to use, whether decorating stone, manuscripts, or metalwork like the hoard. These styles in turn are roughly representative of certain broad dates, although different regions adapted new trends and styles at somewhat different times. The Staffordshire Hoard is representative of Style II zoomorphic art; in filigree as well as in cloisonné, serpentine animal-like creatures adorn the objects with patterns of figure-eight loops and intricate swirls. "Approximate calendar dates . . . would most probably be post-600, and pre-700," according to Karen Høiland Nielsen, an authority on Germanic art at the University of Southern Denmark. Like objects from the Sutton Hoo burial finds, with which they share striking similarities, individual pieces of the hoard reflect a strong Scandinavian influence.

The conspicuous material value of the objects—the gold and garnets—combined with the extraordinary quality of the craftsmanship suggests that the weapons of the hoard constituted elite military equipment. As it happens, the number of swords in the hoard—92 pommels—accords with the number of armed men that it is thought may have made up a nobleman's troop of retainers. The *Anglo-Saxon Chronicle* gives our only citation of such a figure, relating how in 784 "Cyneard slew King Cynewulf, and was slain himself, and eighty-four men with him," the men presumably being Cyneard's companions. Other documentary evidence makes clear that a lord gave and loaned equipment to his followers; one possible explanation of the hoard, then, is that it represents the glittering military gear that once distinguished—and perhaps identified—the retinue of a particular lord.

But why would such elite equipment be broken and buried in the ground?

We have now surveyed some of the ritual beliefs associated with particular features of the multifaceted hoard—beliefs concerning weapons, Christian symbols, the written word, and types of

These gold and garnet scabbard boss fittings are similar to ones found near the hilt of the Sutton Hoo sword. They are thought to have attached the scabbard to the baldric.

This strange conical object is unparalleled, and we can only speculate as to its use.

These garnet-set pyramid sword fittings may have been attached to the straps that held the soldiers' swords in their scabbards. The taller pyramid bears the inverted images of two facing eagles.

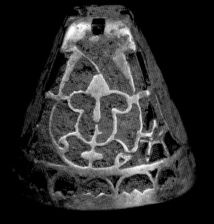

THE ALTAR CROSS

Of the three crosses in the Staffordshire Hoard, the altar cross bears the highest level of artistry. The cross was made up of two sheets of gold fixed together at their edges. One of the sheets bears what looks like deeply cut decoration, but this is deceptive; the metalworker hammered down the surface to give the appearance of deep cutting. The design consists of pairs of interlaced animals, the hind leg of one lying over the face of the other. This motif is similar to one used on metal mounts on wooden bowls in the Sutton Hoo grave, which probably dates to A.D. 625. When found, the arms and shaft of the cross were folded over, and contained between them were five settings that once contained stones, but only one setting survives. Interestingly, this garnet had been repaired in Anglo-Saxon times. Through the sheet metal are a number of nail holes showing that the cross originally had been nailed to a wooden base.

These settings originally held gemstones, only one of which survives.

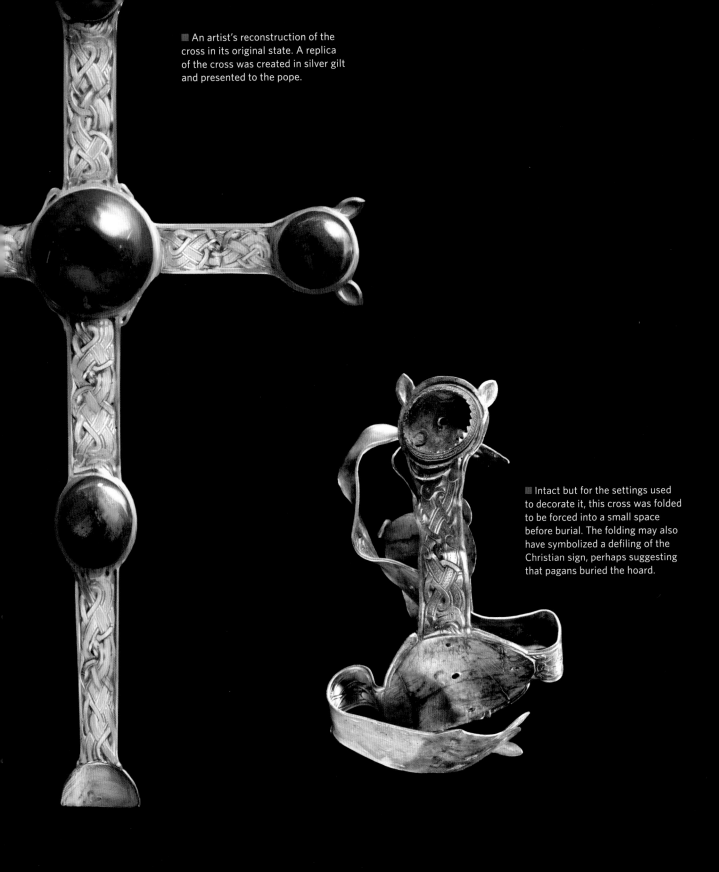

■ An artist's reconstruction of the cross in its original state. A replica of the cross was created in silver gilt and presented to the pope.

■ Intact but for the settings used to decorate it, this cross was folded to be forced into a small space before burial. The folding may also have symbolized a defiling of the Christian sign, perhaps suggesting that pagans buried the hoard.

After Terry Herbert unearthed the initial pieces of the Staffordshire Hoard, Birmingham Archaeology was commissioned to excavate the rest of the treasures. At right, a garnet-inlaid object is pictured in situ, with a coin shown for comparison.

OPPOSITE: A curator at the Birmingham Museum Lab uses modern conservation tools to inspect an ancient treasure. Some experts have estimated that 4x magnification would be needed to create such intricate work today.

ritual deposits that were characteristic of Germanic, as well as Celtic, practice. We have also seen how prevalent hoards of one kind or another are in England, and how they were deposited throughout many different eras. Such a general survey, however, does not tell us why the specific objects of the Staffordshire Hoard might have been buried in the mid- to late seventh century A.D. in farmer Fred Johnson's field.

Now another brief survey of historical events concerning Mercia around the time of the hoard yields some suggestive incidents. The first is described by Bede, our principal

source for this period, and it relates, as so much in Mercia's history does, to the wily King Penda.

Penda, as will be recalled, appears to have spent much of his mortal energy on waging battles with his neighbors near and far. His final, fatal campaign was fought in 655, with Oswiu, the king of Bernicia, a region that today straddles northeast England and southern Scotland. Over the years, Oswiu had been "exposed to the savage and insupportable attacks of Penda, so often mentioned before," according to Bede, who notes that

Penda had previously killed Oswiu's brother. At last Oswiu was forced to promise Penda "an incalculable and incredible store of royal treasures and gifts as the price of peace." Penda, however, refused the offer, and Oswiu, who was Christian,

turned to God's mercy for help seeing that nothing else would save them from this barbarous and evil enemy. Oswiu therefore bound himself with an oath, saying, "If the heathen foe will not accept our gifts, let us offer them to Him who will, even the Lord our God." So he

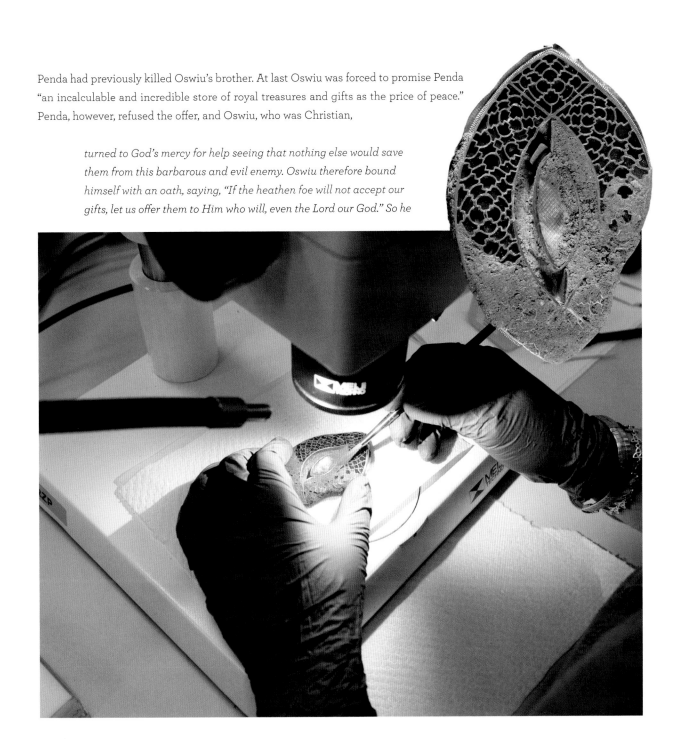

vowed that if he gained the victory he would dedicate his daughter
to the Lord as a holy virgin and give twelve small estates to build
monasteries. In this spirit he entered the fight with his tiny army.

According to Bede, the ensuing battle was "fought near the river Winwæd which, owing to heavy rains, had overflowed its channels and its banks to such an extent that many more were drowned in flight than were destroyed by the sword in battle." Here, on November 15, 655, King Penda fell, and Oswiu, with his tiny army, found himself the improbable victor. Presumably, in the face of so staggering an outcome, Oswiu honored his vow—one hopes his daughter, destined as she now was for a monastery (where, it has to be said, she became a teacher), shared her father's sense of gratitude. Oswiu's vow to dedicate valuable gifts to the god of victory is noteworthy; here it is the Christian God he supplicates, but the practice itself, reminiscent of those described centuries before by the Romans, was also traditionally Germanic. The offer itself of a "king's ransom" in treasure, as established practice, is also noteworthy. Bede's account, then, furnishes us with a historic reason for an assemblage of treasure worthy of a king. That Oswiu dedicated the treasure to God in the event of victory is additionally tantalizing.

A second event concerns a battle fought between Welsh and Mercian forces outside of Lichfield—in other words, in the near vicinity of the Staffordshire Hoard. Event and place are commemorated in a poem, the Welsh *Marwnad Cynddylan,* or "The Death Song of Cynddylan." Cynddylan and his brother Morial were former allies of the ubiquitous Penda in one of his many campaigns, and some scholars believe Cynddylan died with Penda at Winwaed. The poem celebrates Cynddylan's earlier battle, which had ended in a Welsh victory outside of Anglo-Saxon Lichfield:

Grandeur in battle! Extensive spoils
Morial bore off from in front of Lichfield.
Fifteen hundred cattle from the front of battle;
four twenties of stallions and equal harness.
The chief bishop wretched in his four-cornered house,
the book-keeping monks did not protect.
Those who fell in the blood before the splendid warrior
No brother escaped from the entrenchment to his sister.
They escaped from the uproar with grievous wounds.

THE POWER OF GOLD

Gold is found in Britain but only in the Celtic north and west, areas that lay outside of Anglo-Saxon control during the seventh century. The gold in the Staffordshire Hoard is likely to have come from the east, perhaps from the sack of Rome or from Byzantium. Gold was, in the seventh century, much more valuable than it is now. Before the discovery of the rich mines in the New World, the amount of gold in Europe was very limited.

Gold has always been a mystical metal; incorruptible, it is one of the few metals that occurs in a "native" state—that is, as metal rather than an ore that had to be smelted.

Throughout the ages, gold has held powerful sway over the imagination. The ancient Greeks revered Hephaestus, the lame blacksmith whose skill at transforming base metals into gold earned him great renown. Over the centuries people strove to replicate the feat of Hephaestus and transform copper and other base metals into gold through alchemy, a pursuit that generated 4,000 books from the 16th to 18th century that although never finding the fabled magical elixir did lay the foundations of chemistry and pharmacology.

Gold was one of the first metals to be used by humans. Small trinkets made from native metal have been produced since prehistoric times. Gold's luster, heft, rarity and workability further contributed to its powerful place in our imagination.

Gold can be worked like no other material; sheets of it can be beaten so thin that you can see through them. If two pieces of gold are laid together and beaten, they will fuse and become one.

The Staffordshire Hoard shows us what craftsmen can achieve with gold using what must have been the simplest of tools. Saxon craftsmen achieved miracles with filigree, fine gold wires soldered to a surface to form designs, as are shown here. The ease with which pieces of gold can be joined together meant that most objects could be hollow, a great saving of precious metal. A piece of patterned gold foil was placed under each garnet to scatter the light so that the stones glitter. The craftsmen who worked the gold in the hoard were using the metal's amazing workability to maximum effect. ∎

The remarkable fitting from the Staffordshire Hoard may have been fitted to a sword grip. Its amazing filigree decoration is complemented by two garnets forming the eyes of two carefully concealed birds.

Twisted and seemingly wrenched from their original fittings, these garnet-inlaid gold slotted strips may have served as scabbard mounts, book-cover mounts, or saddle fittings.

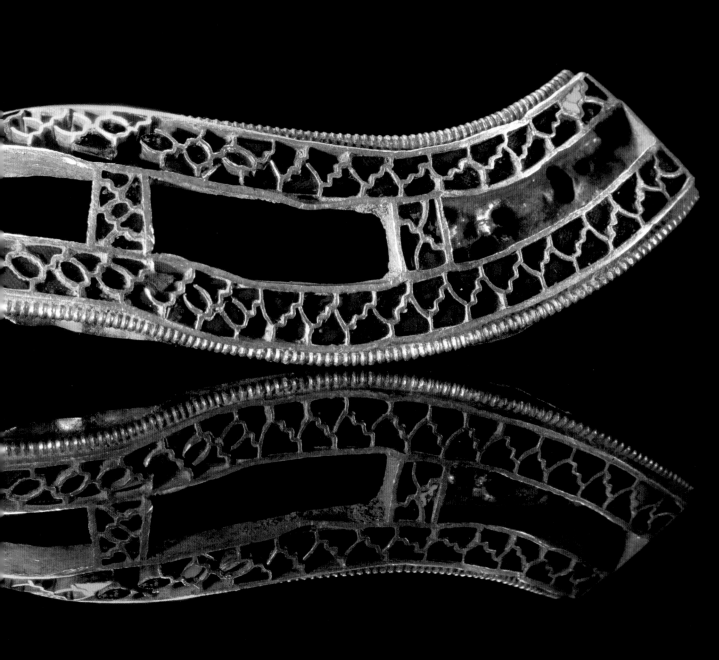

A set of jeweled fittings brightened a hilt of bone or ivory (artist's rendition, below) on a short, light sword known as a seax. A blade of finely patterned iron and steel would have been an integral part of such a weapon, but the treasure mysteriously lacks a single example.

FOLLOWING PAGES: The treasure's flashy ornaments announced the status of men like this aristocrat riding to war.

I shall lament until I would be in my lowly grave plot
for the slaying of Cynndylan, famous to every generous man.

Here, then, in the region of Lichfield, in the mid-seventh century, men had fought a battle from which much plunder was carried away—possibly, for convenience, carried down the old Roman road that led past the find spot of the Staffordshire Hoard. The plunder included, it would seem, loot of some kind from a "wretched" bishop, a detail that inevitably conjures the presence of the two gold crosses in the Staffordshire Hoard.

Historic literature thus suggests several reasons why a miscellany of expensive military equipment might have been assembled: It was ransom of sorts, blood money to buy off a predatory battle-lord. Or it was war spoil, collected from a broken army.

LOST GOLD OF THE DARK AGES

An artist's vision of a helmet from the time of the treasure *(opposite page)* could have included the intricately worked cheek panel found in the hoard *(this page)*. It is embellished with three friezes of running, interlaced animals, a typical Anglo-Saxon motif.

One historian has interpreted the hoard as the actual ransom offered by Oswiu to Penda and brought back with him after his unexpected victory in the north to be buried in the Mercian heartland, which he now possessed, perhaps for safekeeping, perhaps as a dedicatory offering for the victory. When in the same year Welsh forces defeated the Mercians outside of Lichfield (or maybe, as allies of the Mercians, defeated a Northumbrian army), the owners of the buried treasure may have died in battle, and the hoard languished unclaimed. There are other, less attractive and tidy explanations too. The hoard may have been expensive scrap metal, for example, a royal goldsmith's assembly of material that was never retrieved.

It is the gold that dazzles. But in practical terms the most valuable part of the most valuable weapon—the sword—is not in fact represented in the hoard. As desirable as the ornate pommels and pommel guards may have been, the part of the sword any warrior would have coveted, as one historian has remarked acidly, was "the long sharp pointy bit you killed people with." Presumably the iron and steel of the double-edged swords and single-bladed seaxes from which the pommels were stripped remained with the party that deposited the treasure.

How was the value of the hoard assessed in its own time? In terms of its *solidi* value? Its symbolism? The rank of its former owner, or how the treasure was lost or won? And if we had the hard facts, could we "understand" them? The hoard and its perplexing burial belong to a world in which even mundane events were suffused with magic and spiritual meaning. Gold had magic properties; and garnets too, those stones the color of blood, may also have been "charged." Art historians believe that the enigmatic animal figures that writhe and coil decoratively over so much Anglo-Saxon art could also

FOLLOWING PAGES: A detailed view of the finely carved animals on the gold cheekpiece. Intricately rendered zoomorphic themes run throughout many of the pieces of the Staffordshire Hoard.

The Death Song of Cynddylan

The Anglo-Saxons wrote outstanding poetry like *Beowulf*, but the Welsh too had a tradition of celebrating their heroes in verse. One of these poems, "The Death Song of Cynddylan," refers to Lichfield, Mercia's ecclesiastical center and home to Lichfield Cathedral. Dating to the middle of the seventh century, the poem was written around the time and place of the burial of the Staffordshire Hoard. Cynddylan ap Cyndrwyn ("cun-thu-lan," son of Cyndrwyn) was possibly king of Powys in Wales. One of these poems tells us that Cynddylan was present at the Battle of Maserfelth (August 6, 642), at which King Penda defeated and killed Oswald of Northumbria, and this gives us a date for Cynddylan's activities. A haunting poem, "The Death Song of Cynddylan" contains some tantalizing lines:

> *Before Lichfield they fought,*
> *There was gore under ravens*
> *and keen attack.*
> *Limed shields broke before the sons*
> *of the Cyndrwynyn [Cyndrwyn]*

The original Welsh text refers to Caer Lwytgoed, the old Roman town of Letocetum—the Grey Wood, or Wall as it is now known, just three miles down Watling Street from where the hoard was found. Further details of the battle are given:

> *Grandeur in battle! Extensive spoils*
> *Morial bore off from in front*
> *of Lichfield.*
> *Fifteen hundred cattle from*
> *the front of battle;*
> *four twenties of stallions and*
> *equal harness.*
> *The chief bishop wretched in his*
> *four-cornered house (?),*
> *the book-keeping monks*
> *did not protect.*
> *Those who fell in the blood before*
> *the splendid warrior*

While the passage describes the kind of circumstances that may have led to the deposit of the Staffordshire Hoard, with its references to "stallions and equal harness" and "the book-keeping monks," it would be naive to suggest any link between the verse and the hoard. However, the hoard was found in the frontier zone between the Anglo-Saxons and the Welsh, and the latter are likely to have played a part in the foundation of Mercia. At the Battle of Hatfield Chase in 633 Penda fought as an ally of Cadwallon. Given the shifting political alliances of seventh-century Mercia, it is not surprising that a hoard may have been buried for reasons of secrecy, safety, or simply storage, and then abandoned. ■

have been magic; used on weapons, these designs may have been apotropaic and, like the armor and weapons themselves, intended to turn away or ward off harm. Not only individual elements—the goldsmith's raw materials and his chosen iconography—but the very art of metallurgy was informed by magic. Odin's spear and gold ring, Thor's hammer, Frija's necklace—in Nordic sagas these attributes of the gods were the handiwork of magic, created by dwarfish blacksmiths who toiled underground. Here, as in many cultures, the blacksmith is associated with taboo and magic, and is himself a mystical figure.

It is unlikely that we will ever know the story of the Staffordshire Hoard; and if the hoard did serve some mystical purpose, it is perhaps appropriate that we will not. The potent magic of treasure laid with deliberate carefulness in the ground is conjured best by the great Anglo-Saxon epic *Beowulf*, which so wonderfully straddles two ages and two worlds— Nordic pagan and Anglo-Saxon Christian, Scandinavian and English, the way the world was and the way it was becoming. The epic, we recall, culminates in the death of the now aged hero Beowulf. Fighting a dragon, the old warrior is mortally wounded, and both dragon and warrior die. The treasure the dragon loyally guarded—the hoard—is exposed to gawking eyes:

> That huge cache, gold inherited
> from an ancient race, was under a spell—
> which meant no one was ever permitted
> to enter the ring-hall unless God Himself,
> Mankind's Keeper, True King of Triumph,
> allowed some person pleasing to Him—
> and in his eyes worthy—to open the hoard.

The exposure of the treasure signals that the old order is drawing to a close. With this realization, the dragon itself is recalled with sudden, unexpected nostalgia: "He had shimmered forth / on the night air once, then winged back / down to his den; but death owned him now, he would never enter his earth-gallery again."

This stylized and diminutive gold animal measuring just 1.6 inches high is notable for the fineness of its filigree. Its exact use is unknown, though it must have decorated a larger object.

CHAPTER SIX

THE LAST BATTLE

"I remembered also that I saw, before it had been all ravaged and burned, how the churches throughout the whole of England stood filled with treasures and books,"

— KING ALFRED

THE LAST BATTLE

I n A.D. 737, St. Boniface, who had been born in Wessex, wrote home from Germany to implore all who were "sprung from the stock and race of the English" to support his missionary work among the Germanic heathens. "Have pity on them," he wrote of his constituency, "because even they themselves are wont to say: 'We are of one blood and one bone.'"

A close identification with the German homelands informed early Anglo-Saxon sensibilities and accounted for the particular desire of the English Church to convert its heathen kin on the Continent. Bishop Torhthelm of the Mercian town of Leicester, for example, wrote to Boniface to congratulate him for his labors on the behalf of *gens nostra*—"our race"—while St. Aldhelm, who was related to the king of Wessex, similarly refers to "our stock" and "the Germanic race." The identification was expressed in numerous ways, as seen, such as the perpetuation of Germanic heroic values expressed in poetry and song, as well as actual deeds, and the determination of Anglo-Saxon kings to trace their genealogies to a Germanic past.

At the same time, once in possession of Britannia, the Germanic barbarians and their descendants showed a remarkable affinity for the cultural legacy of Rome—the Latin language, the literature, the architecture, and the symbols of imperial authority. When the Roman Empire had held sway, the Rhine and the Danube had served to delineate not only territorial boundaries—the extent of Rome's domain—but also boundaries of civilization. The Germanic tribes north and east of these great

OPPOSITE: Site of the Vikings' second major raid in Britain in 794, Jarrow Monastery had been home to the scholar and monk Saint Bede. It was destroyed by the Danes in 860 and abandoned by the end of the century.

PREVIOUS PAGES: Royal seat of the Saxon kings of Northumbria, Bamburgh Castle was destroyed by Vikings in 993 and rebuilt under Norman rule.

LOST GOLD OF THE DARK AGES

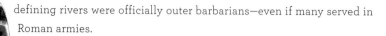

defining rivers were officially outer barbarians—even if many served in Roman armies.

But while still retaining and honoring a keen awareness of their Germanic origins following their conversion, the Anglo-Saxons adopted what survived of the culture of Rome, now mostly in the caretaking of the church. Within a hundred years of Augustine's arrival in Kent for missionary duties, Anglo-Saxon monasteries had established renowned scriptoria and were enhancing their own libraries. Bede knew the works of Pliny, and Alcuin the works of Virgil. Anglo-Saxon pilgrims to Rome encountered the most striking remnants of imperial might, but there were Roman ruins to contemplate in their own land as well: St. Cuthbert, according to an anonymous biographer, was in 685 shown the walls of the town of Carlisle, "formerly built in a wonderful manner by the Romans." Anglo-Saxon rulers seeking to convey their kingly status grasped at Roman symbols and practices. When the Anglo-Saxons began producing their own coinage, for example, they naturally copied the most successful currency the world had known. A penny struck for the East Anglian king Æthelberht at the end of the eighth century bore an image of Romulus and Remus, while coins of King Offa of Mercia depicted the king robed and crowned with a diadem in imperial style.

Anglo-Saxon culture, then, was a fusion of old Germanic and Roman—or Romano-British—culture, informed and shaped by Christianity. And while the Anglo-Saxons themselves looked to the inhabitants of their continental homelands with interest and compassion, they were aware that they themselves were no longer Saxons or Angles, Frisians or Jutes, but something other—Mercians and Northumbrians and West Saxons, for example. English identity as such did not yet exist, and it was the appearance of another Nordic-Germanic people on Anglo-Saxon soil that helped sharpen the sense of common identity.

The Vikings: Their name first appears in Old English in the late-seventh-century poem *Widsith,* as *Wicinga cynn,* the race of the Vikings. The word is thought to derive from the Vik, the bay area in southeastern Norway, believed to have been an important maritime region. Coming from homelands lying in modern Norway and Denmark, they were sea pirates, raiding coastal and river communities for plunder in their swift, shallow-hulled boats. In A.D. 787, according to the *Anglo-Saxon Chronicle,* "came first three ships of the Northmen from the land of robbers." Landing in Portland, in Dorset, their visit resulted in the death of the local sheriff, who in his innocence greeted "the Danish

This silver penny shows Æthelberht (d. A.D. 794) as a Roman emperor and has Romulus and Remus on its reverse, clearly linking back to imperial times.

OPPOSITE: The Cuerdale hoard was buried around 905, probably by Vikings from Ireland. Its 88 pounds of silver came from Ireland, England, Europe, and the Arab world, demonstrating the Vikings' wide-ranging contacts.

men," who presumably went on to carry out a raid. But the Vikings storm into history, so to speak, on June 8, 793, with their sack of the Lindisfarne monastery on the Holy Island.

Initially the Vikings came only for portable plunder; then, perhaps like the Saxons and Angles before them, they realized that land, and with it power, was also for the taking. By the mid-ninth century, they were not only sacking, but also occupying and controlling whole regions of Britain. In 867, they put the Northumbrian city of York to the torch and its king, Aelle, to their "blood eagle" ordeal, ripping out his ribs and lungs as a living sacrifice to Odin.

"I remembered also that I saw, before it had been all ravaged and burned, how the churches throughout the whole of England stood filled with treasures and books," recalled King Alfred, writing in the late ninth century. In 870, after taking Northumbria, the Viking army "rode over Mercia into East Anglia," according to the *Anglo-Saxon*

THE VIKINGS

A growing population in Scandinavia, pressures from the Carolingian Empire, and the vulnerability of areas overseas are all likely to have played a part in precipitating the Viking raids of the eighth century. Scandinavian longships and expert seamanship made possible open-sea crossings, allowing Vikings to reach North America and to sail into the Mediterranean. One group founded a kingdom on the Volga, which was named after them—the Rus (sia).

The earliest raids, such as the attack on Lindisfarne in 793, were small-scale, despite the outrage they caused. Later Viking armies led by kings campaigned and wintered in England, bent on conquest, not loot. Despite their rapacious reputation, the Vikings were heavily involved in trade: Silk has been found at Lincoln and York, and Arab silver coins in England show Viking links with Baghdad and the Muslim world. In the late ninth century, King Alfred halted the conquest of England, thus forcing the Vikings to settle for only half the country, thereafter known as the Danelaw. In the 11th century, Cnut conquered the whole of England, which then formed part of his transient Danish empire.

In 1066 England was conquered by the Normans, another Viking people, who had adopted French as their language. The Viking legacy in England included many common words from Danish, as well as place-names ending in -by and -thorpe that show where Vikings settled. Finds of small metal objects by metal-detector hobbyists like Terry Herbert, discoverer of the Staffordshire Hoard, are making important contributions to our knowledge of the Vikings. It was once thought that, with the exception of some carved stones, no archaeological evidence existed for them in England. But now large numbers of these metal objects decorated in Viking style, such as brooches and strap fittings, present another picture. Most of these finds are of poor quality, indicating that ordinary Scandinavians moved to England, not just the aristocratic leadership. ∎

A detailed Viking runestone from Tjanguide, Alskog, Gottland, showing a Viking ship

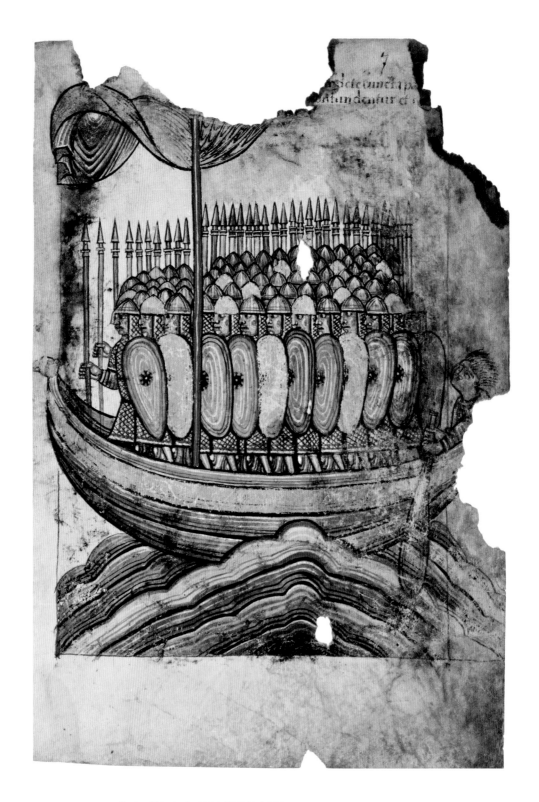

LOST GOLD OF THE DARK AGES

Chronicle. That winter, King Edmund met them, "but the Danes gained the victory and slew the king; whereupon they overran all the land, and destroyed all the monasteries to which they came." The following year, the army rode into Wessex, now the only kingdom they had not taken, where they were confronted by King Aethelred and his younger brother, Alfred. After several inconclusive campaigns that year, which also saw the death of Aethelred, Alfred, at the age of 22, became king of Wessex.

Over the ensuing seven years, Alfred and his Wessex army fought the Vikings in a relentless series of intensifying, but still inconclusive, battles. At last, in spring 878, Alfred won a decisive victory at the Battle of Edington, in Wiltshire. In war, the young king had proved himself to be a skilled and determined warrior, and in victory he was to prove a statesman. In a move that was at once strategically brilliant and desperately risky, Alfred made a pact with Guthrum, the Viking king. Three weeks later, according to the *Anglo-Saxon Chronicle,* "King Guthrum, attended by some thirty of the worthiest men that were in the army, came to [Alfred] at Aller, which is near Athelney, and there the king became his sponsor in baptism."

With the baptism of the Viking king, Alfred had won a moral as well as martial victory. Under Guthrum, the Vikings left Wessex and eventually settled in East Anglia, where they lived more or less peacefully. The Danelaw was established—a huge swath of Britain, encompassing Northumbria, East Anglia, and part of Mercia, which was mutually recognized as being under Danish law. Still, sporadic raids continued, with new ships arriving from Denmark, and Anglo-Saxon England was never again wholly free of the Viking menace. The Anglo-Danish population, like that of the Romano-Britons and the British Anglo-Saxons before them, would leave their distinctive mark on the evolving nation. This is seen, for example, in the concentration of place-names ending in -by, meaning "village"—Wetherby, Grimsby, Crosby—in the Danish territories known as the Five Boroughs, or the fortified towns of Lincoln, Stamford, Derby, Leicester, and Nottingham.

Decorated with an interlaced animal inlaid in silver, this Viking iron axe from Mammen in Denmark dates between 960 and 1012. The animal's Scandinavian ancestors included creatures like those seen in the Staffordshire Hoard.

OPPOSITE: This 11th-century French painting from *La Vie de Saint Aubin d'Angers* depicts Norman invaders crossing the English Channel.

At the time of the coming of the Vikings, England had been divided into its several unequal kingdoms, including Northumbria, or the land north of the River Humber; Mercia in the Midlands; East Anglia, or the land of the Angles, to the east; and the West Saxon lands, or Wessex. Each kingdom had been formed by the consolidation of smaller tribes, chiefdoms, and even other kingdoms, acquired sometimes through alliances but mostly by battle. There had been powerful, wide-ruling kings before Alfred; Offa of Mercia, for example, had ruled all land south of the Humber and had termed himself Rex Anglorum—King of the Angles. But they remained more or less local figures, with their self-identification and outlooks rooted in their particular kingdoms. In this respect they represented particularly successful examples of the traditional Germanic lord.

But now, following his historic victory at Edington, Alfred was the first to warrant the title "King of England." In A.D. 887, the *Anglo-Saxon Chronicle* records, "the whole English nation turned to him, except that part of it which was held captive by the Danes." Here, a note of caution must be sounded regarding that uniquely valuable, much-relied-upon document, the *Anglo-Saxon Chronicle* itself, the earlier parts of which were put together from a number of lost sources around 892, in Wessex—compiled, in other words, during Alfred's reign. Consequently, we know a great deal more about Wessex and Alfred the Great than of any other kingdom or king, and the representation that the eyes of a grateful and now unified nation turned instinctively toward the king of Wessex must be taken at something less than face value. This said, the fact remains that Alfred's victories against a foreign foe had implications for people beyond his own now very powerful kingdom. The Viking threat had thrown into disarray the old assemblage of independent kingdoms and, at the least, enforced a broad awareness that the *Angel Cynn*—or English people of Angle land, or England—were collectively vulnerable to overseas invasion, and in this awareness can be seen a seed of national identity.

The same year in which Alfred was hailed as king of England also saw, according to the *Anglo-Saxon Chronicle*, his fortification of the city of London. London was not only the largest and most important city in all of England, but also the principal town of Mercia, and Alfred's refurbishment of the city should be seen as an expression of the authority of Wessex over an old rival, as well as a remarkable public work. The grid of streets he lay out within the restored city walls would endure for nearly eight centuries, or until the Great Fire of London in 1666, while its influence has endured to the present day.

LOST GOLD OF THE DARK AGES

THE LAST BATTLE

THE ANGLO-SAXON LEGACY

The Anglo-Saxon–dominated chapter of Britain's history lasted for over 650 years—from A.D. 410, when Rome withdrew, until the Norman Conquest in 1066. After this long history, what aspects of the Britain we know can be traced back to the Angles and Saxons?

The English language would appear to be the greatest lasting contribution, but English has changed substantially since the Anglo-Saxon (also called Old English) of the Dark Ages. Under the Vikings it incorporated bits of Old Norse and then changed even more with Norman French. However, modern English is distinctly rooted in Old English. It is notable that all of the main farmyard animals—cow, sheep, and pig—have English names, but the words for their meat—beef, mutton, and pork—are all French, showing who was rearing livestock and who was getting to eat it. Old English literature gives us some of the earliest records of English society, through such classics as *Beowulf;* the Lindisfarne Gospels; poems, law codes, wills, and charters; and the *Anglo-Saxon Chronicle.*

English religious rankings and church districts arose during the earliest years of English Christianity. The Archbishoprics of Canterbury and York predate the English monarchy by hundreds of years. The redistricting of dioceses by Theodore of Tarsus in the 670s and 680s laid the foundations for the Church of England.

The strongest and longest-lasting Anglo-Saxon legacy, however, lies in government institutions, which the Normans left intact. The British Parliament originated in two Anglo-Saxon traditions: the *witan,* a king's advisory council, which evolved into the House of Lords; and the *moots*—regular shire, or county, meetings—which inspired the House of Commons. The Anglo-Saxons also established regional governments in the shires, further divided into hundreds and tithings. Courts were held regularly, with oath-givers, like juries, that helped establish guilt or innocence. These were the foundations of English Common Law that later spread around the world with the British Empire. ■

The Alfred Jewel honors King Alfred, who had a long-ranging impact on England.

The restoration of London was only part of a grand and farsighted plan that extended to the defense of Wessex, now the base of England's authority and power. Alfred strategically established a network of *burhs*, or fortified towns and settlements, throughout the length and breadth of southern England. No inhabited settlement was more than one day's march, or 20 miles, from the safety of these strongholds. An estimated 27,000 laborers were conscripted for the execution of this audacious plan, which required thousands of tons of paving flint and miles of walls, ditches, and palisades, while some rivers—which had provided the Vikings with such ready access—were barred with defensive stations on either bank. Excavations have revealed the careful town planning that went

An illustration depicts the great Battle of Brunanburh in 937.

FOLLOWING PAGES: The skeletal branches of a tree hang over Senlac Hill in Sussex, where the Battle of Hastings raged in 1066.

THE LAST BATTLE

LOST GOLD OF THE DARK AGES

into the construction of the burhs and have shown that they were not intended merely as safe havens where refugees could huddle in times of danger, but also as places to be inhabited and settled and developed. In later times, many would become centers of trade and royal mints—important elements of the infrastructure of wide governance.

According to the traditional, romantic story line, England was forged from Alfred's victories over the Vikings. In fact, both during Alfred's reign and for some time afterward, fully half of England was officially in Danish hands. The creation of unified England is more properly credited to Alfred's grandson, Æthelstan, whose serial victories, from Scotland in the north to Wales in the west to Cornwall in the south culminated in his being recognized, in 926, as not only Rex Anglorum but also emperor of the world of Britain. This seemingly definitive landmark in England's history was in turn overtaken and overturned by subsequent events, which saw more wars waged between both old and new factions. Even to skim the entries of the *Anglo-Saxon Chronicle* is to conjure

The Normans had a major impact on the English landscape. They rebuilt churches and cathedrals, including the Durham Cathedral, pictured in this 19th-century illustration.

OPPOSITE: William the Conqueror kills King Harold Godwinson at the Battle of Hastings, from the medieval *Decrees of Kings of Anglo-Saxon and Norman England.*

THE DOMESDAY BOOK

Unique in Europe, the Domesday Survey was ordered by William the Conqueror at Christmas 1085 and completed with amazing efficiency the following year. Although the commissioners appear to have counted everything, this is deceptive: William was interested only in learning who owned what land, how much revenue it generated each year, and how much wealth he could grab for himself. The document looks simple and straightforward; it is written in abbreviated Latin, and each entry follows a set formula. But the survey is in fact highly complex and ambiguous. In addition to figures for 1086, it also quotes figures for 1066. These indicate a fall in revenue in the intervening years, with large areas described as "waste," some of which was likely due to the trauma of the Norman Conquest. Certainly the names of the landowners show that changes had taken place. By 1086 very few of the large landowners were Anglo-Saxon; they had been replaced by Normans who had come across with William. Although land was the main asset recorded, the commissioners looked at everything of economic interest: woodland, meadow, grazing land (for hogs), plow teams (of eight oxen each, without which the land was valueless), mills, churches, fisheries, and ironworks—all were counted. Then there were the people. The Domesday Survey was not a census—it counted only heads of households—but we can get an idea of their status, since *villeins* (peasants), *sokemen* (freeholders), and *servi* (slaves) were all mentioned.

William found that the annual value of England in 1086 was about £73,000, not all of which would have been in coins; much would have been in goods. The only coin in use at the time was the silver penny, and, while it is difficult to make comparison, it was probably equivalent to about nine dollars. William took 15 percent of the national income for himself—twice as much as his predecessor. ∎

Compiled for William the Conqueror between 1086 and 1090, the Domesday Book recorded all owners of land and property in England.

a chronic state of turbulence: "This year King Æthelstan and Edmund his brother led a force to Brunanburh," states the chronicle for the year 937, nearly a decade after the ratification of an agreement between Æthelstan and the other kings of the island; "and there fought against Olaf; and, Christ helping, had the victory: and they there slew five kings and seven earls." Nor were the Viking depredations of Alfred's late ninth century by any means the last England was to see of Danish and other Scandinavian invaders. For nearly two decades in the early 11th century, Cnut, a prince and later king of Denmark, was king of all England.

The official end of the Anglo-Saxon era can be dated with exactness to Saturday, October 14, 1066. This was the day on which William, Duke of Normandy, having sailed across the English Channel with an army of Norman and mercenary forces, confronted the English army under Harold Godwinson, king of England. Until a generation before the invasion, Normandy had been a Viking province, and its leaders the *Duces Northmannorum*—Leaders of the Northmen. The Viking Northmen, however, had embraced French culture with what seems to have been great facility and ardor, and by the time of the invasion they were French in all but genealogy. Linked to the English royal family through Emma, his great aunt, William saw the invasion of 1066 as his rightful claim—backed by the pope—to the throne of England.

In autumn 1066, King Harold was in York, and he had just celebrated a hard-fought victory over an invading Norwegian army when he received word of William's invasion. Rushing south, Harold, and possibly as little as a third of his army, met William and the Normans near Hastings, in Sussex. The Battle of Hastings commenced in the morning and concluded at dusk, with William and the Normans victorious and King Harold hacked brutally to death.

"William the earl landed at Hastings, on St. Michael's-day: and Harold came from the north, and fought against

King William Rufus, who ruled from 1087 to 1100. Known for his ruddy complexion, flamboyance, and ruthlessness, Rufus was unloved by his subjects.

him, before all his army had come up: and there he fell, and his two brothers, Girth and Leofwin; and William subdued this land. And he came to Westminster, and Archbishop Aldred consecrated him king." Thus the *Anglo-Saxon Chronicle* succinctly records the passing of England from Anglo-Saxon into Norman hands.

Today, throughout the length and breadth of the kingdom, visible relics of England's remarkable hybrid history survive. In the county of Staffordshire, for example, one can still see fragments of the vanished, once-powerful kingdom of Mercia. Odds and ends of Anglo-Saxon life, such as traces of the town's defenses and a water mill, have been found in Tamworth, the capital of Mercia, where a statue stands to LadyAethelflaed, King Alfred's daughter, who ruled Mercia in the early tenth century before it was incorporated into a united kingdom of England. Repairs made to the nave of the medieval cathedral of Lichfield, once the Mercian episcopal see, recently brought to light a carved angel from Offa's ninth century. In Repton, where the *Anglo-Saxon Chronicle* records the burial of the murdered King Æthelbald of Mercia in 757, the vaulted crypt of St. Wystan's Church dates to the ninth century. The modern A5 roadway now follows the route of Watling Street, the Roman road that once took the unknown travelers and their sack of gold to wherever they were traveling. The remote heathland where the travelers buried the gold today supports vegetables, horses, and cattle. The Staffordshire Hoard itself can be seen in the Birmingham Museums and Art Gallery and the Stoke-on-Trent Potteries Museum—both established in what was Mercian territory.

An elegy delivered for the hero Beowulf makes a fitting tribute to the robust, bloody, and epochal Anglo-Saxon age: "So it is goodbye now to all you know and love / on your home ground," says Wiglaf, faithful companion who stood by the aged Beowulf until his death; "the open-handedness, / the giving of war swords. Every one of you / with freeholds of land, our whole nation, / will be dispossessed."

THE STAFFORDSHIRE HOARD

KEVIN LEAHY

The Staffordshire Hoard has been a revelation to everyone involved. Both the quantity and the quality of the material are stunning. Conservation and cleaning of the finds is under way, and as layers of earth are painstakingly removed, animals and faces are appearing under the microscope. Archaeologists are now beginning to place the finds in their Anglo-Saxon context by comparing them with earlier discoveries and making links with sites like Sutton Hoo in Suffolk. The images that follow, some of which are appearing for the first time, give an impression of what has been found and the upcoming challenges, including conservation; scientific analysis; and making this remarkable material available through books, broadcasts, and museum displays.

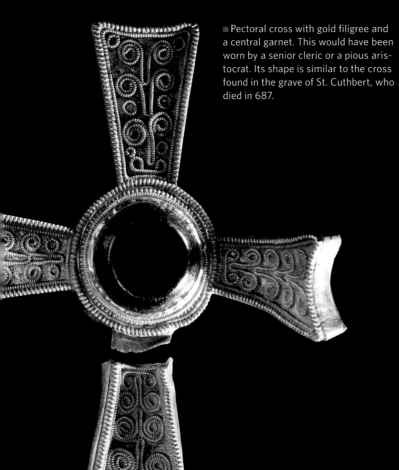

■ Pectoral cross with gold filigree and a central garnet. This would have been worn by a senior cleric or a pious aristocrat. Its shape is similar to the cross found in the grave of St. Cuthbert, who died in 687.

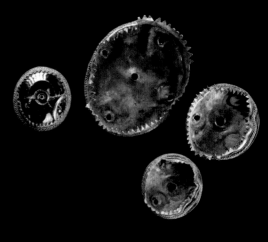

■ Settings for gems from the processional cross, opposite. Only one setting retains a gem—a garnet damaged and repaired in Anglo-Saxon times.

■ Strip of metal, perhaps the arm of a cross. At one end is an empty D-shaped setting. On both faces is a biblical inscription from the Book of Numbers.

■ Altar, or processional cross, made from thin sheet gold with chased decoration, now folded and bent. Its decoration is similar to that seen on metal mounts from the early seventh-century Sutton Hoo ship burial.

■ L-shaped gold strip with fine garnet settings covering three faces. The function of this object is unknown, but it may have come from the cover of a book.

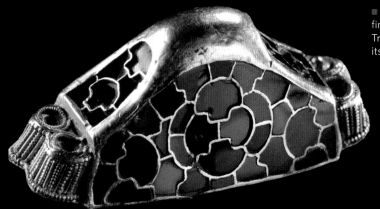

■ Pommel cap decorated with finely cut geometric garnets. Traces of wear can be seen on its top.

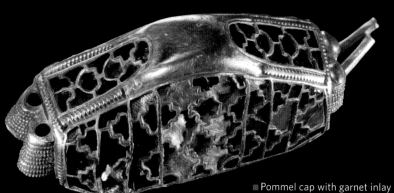

■ Pommel cap with garnet inlay but with some of the cells blanked off with gold plates, a technique known as lidded cloisonné.

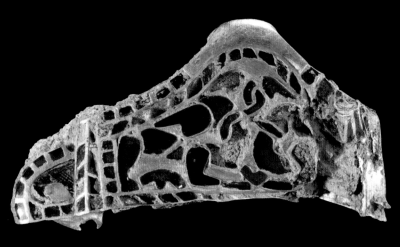

■ Cap decorated with lidded cloisonné representing two crossing animals. A foot can be seen to the right of the vertical bar.

■ Pommel cap decorated with garnets forming a winged disk. These round-topped caps may be later in the series than the more common cocked hat type.

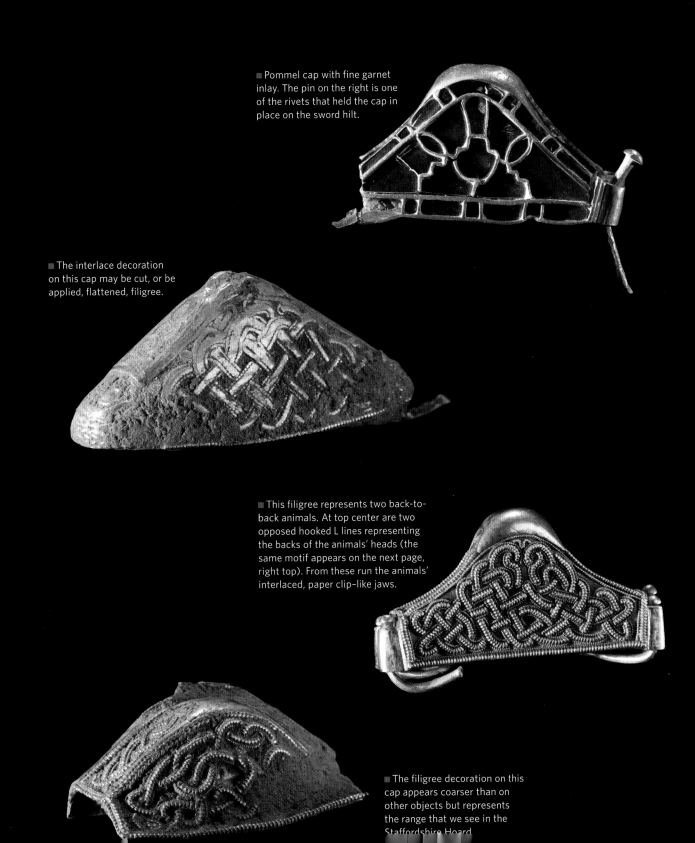

■ Pommel cap with fine garnet inlay. The pin on the right is one of the rivets that held the cap in place on the sword hilt.

■ The interlace decoration on this cap may be cut, or be applied, flattened, filigree.

■ This filigree represents two back-to-back animals. At top center are two opposed hooked L lines representing the backs of the animals' heads (the same motif appears on the next page, right top). From these run the animals' interlaced, paper clip–like jaws.

■ The filigree decoration on this cap appears coarser than on other objects but represents the range that we see in the Staffordshire Hoard.

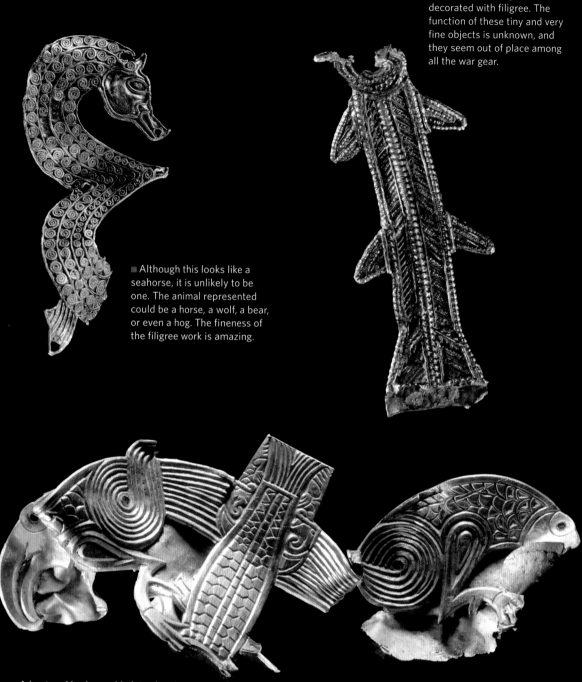

■ Fish made from gold and decorated with filigree. The function of these tiny and very fine objects is unknown, and they seem out of place among all the war gear.

■ Although this looks like a seahorse, it is unlikely to be one. The animal represented could be a horse, a wolf, a bear, or even a hog. The fineness of the filigree work is amazing.

■ A bent and broken gold plate showing two birds of prey clutching a fish (center). One bird's hooked beak can be seen on the left. Behind it is a shield-shaped panel marking its hip, from which extend the talons. This object may have been fitted on a shield.

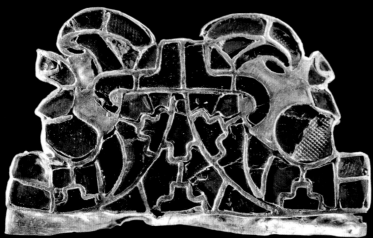

Garnet inlaid plate representing two eagles. In its center, the backs of the eagles' heads are marked by the two back-to-back L-shaped stones from which the hooked beaks extend. One stone (center right) is missing, revealing the waffle-patterned foil set beneath. These foils scattered the light and made the stone glitter.

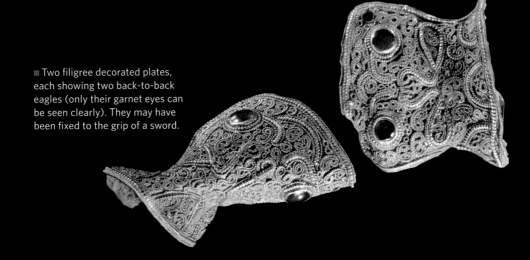

Two filigree decorated plates, each showing two back-to-back eagles (only their garnet eyes can be seen clearly). They may have been fixed to the grip of a sword.

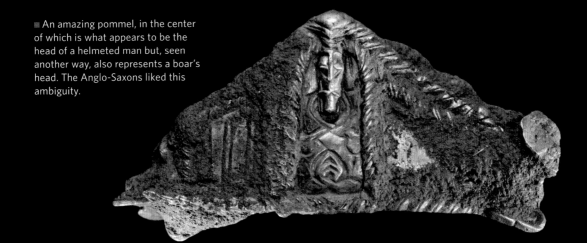

An amazing pommel, in the center of which is what appears to be the head of a helmeted man but, seen another way, also represents a boar's head. The Anglo-Saxons liked this ambiguity.

■ Silver gilt cheekpiece from a helmet decorated with rows of animals, some of which have the L-shaped line at the backs of their heads (see detail, inset). The section of this object is like half a seashell with a raised flange down one side.

Crest fittings from an Anglo-Saxon helmet. The crest was fitted into a channeled strip, hook-shaped on the illustration. Its decoration is similar to that of the cheekpiece, suggesting that they came from the same helmet. The horse-head terminal fits into one end of the channeled strip.

■ Foil showing running or kneeling warriors, each carrying a round shield and a spear and with a sword at his side. Their heads are thrown back to look upward, with their hair streaming out behind them.

■ Foil showing a procession of animals, their circular eyes and V-shaped jaws at the top of the strip.

Foil showing the faces of two mustached warriors.

Detail of the channeled strip that held the helmet crest (see page 217), showing four inter-laced snakes.

At Sutton Hoo, small gold buckles like this were found with the helmet.

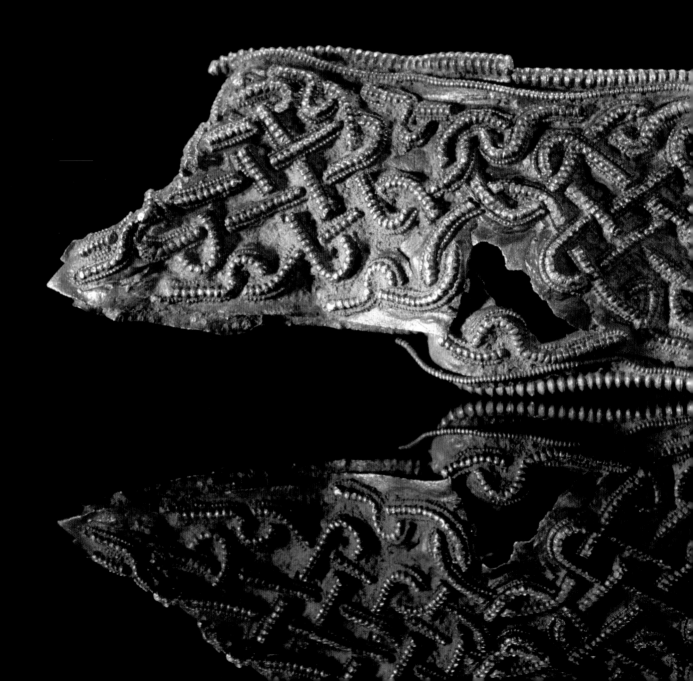

This fine filigree shows something of the sophistication of the technique. Each strand making up the interlaced animals consists of a length of beaded wire flanked by two smaller wires. These were skillfully soldered onto the gold backing plate to create a design of great delicacy.

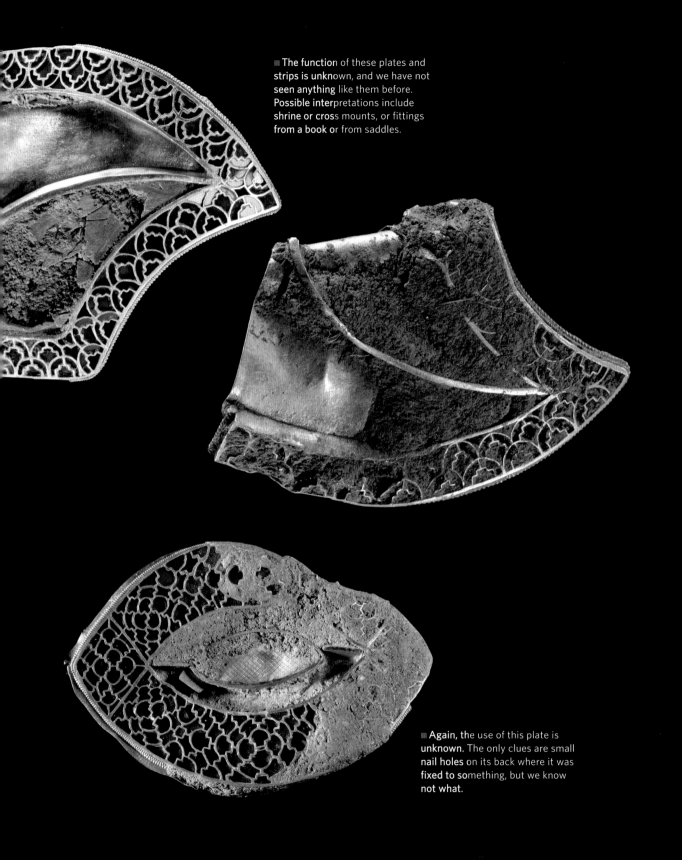

■ The function of these plates and strips is unknown, and we have not seen anything like them before. Possible interpretations include shrine or cross mounts, or fittings from a book or from saddles.

■ Again, the use of this plate is unknown. The only clues are small nail holes on its back where it was fixed to something, but we know not what.

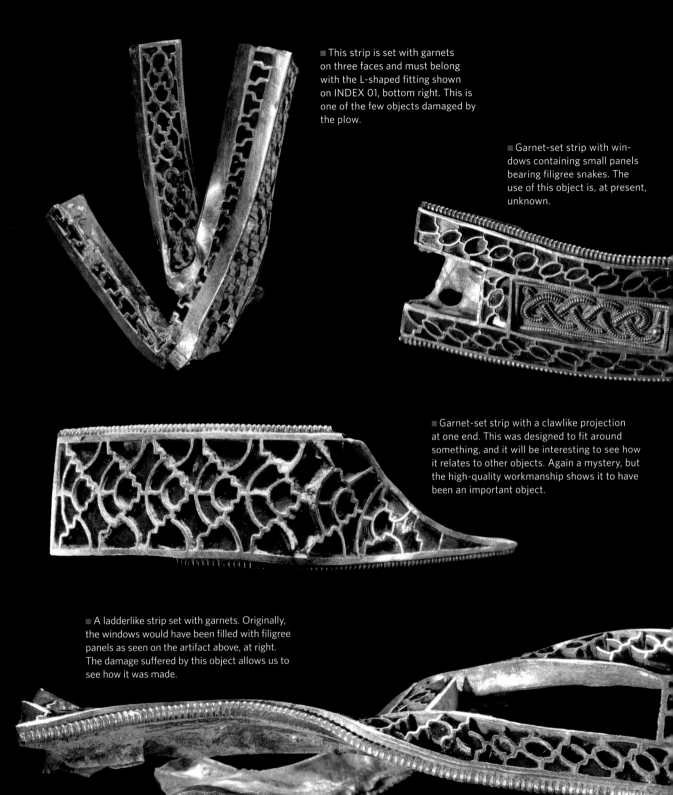

■ This strip is set with garnets on three faces and must belong with the L-shaped fitting shown on INDEX 01, bottom right. This is one of the few objects damaged by the plow.

■ Garnet-set strip with windows containing small panels bearing filigree snakes. The use of this object is, at present, unknown.

■ Garnet-set strip with a clawlike projection at one end. This was designed to fit around something, and it will be interesting to see how it relates to other objects. Again a mystery, but the high-quality workmanship shows it to have been an important object.

■ A ladderlike strip set with garnets. Originally, the windows would have been filled with filigree panels as seen on the artifact above, at right. The damage suffered by this object allows us to see how it was made.

■ Two gold and garnet sword buttons. At Sutton Hoo buttons like these were found in situ on one face of the scabbard and were likely to have been used to attach it to a belt.

■ Two sword-hilt rings bearing garnets with grooved decoration. The upper ring had lost one of its garnets, which had been replaced with amber.

■ Hilt plate decorated with biting animals similar to some seen on the seventh-century Book of Durrow. The slot for the blade has one square-cut end showing that this plate was used on a single-edged seax.

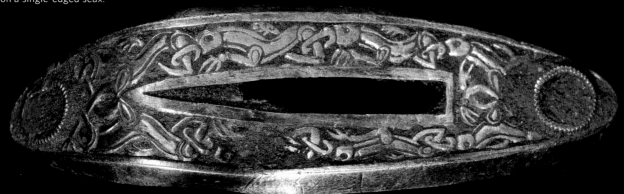

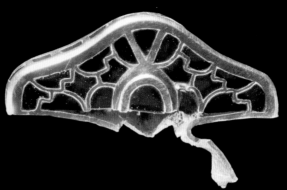

These elegant fittings are decorated with similar lidded cloisonné animals and must have formed a set. They are mounts not for a sword, but for a single-edged seax.

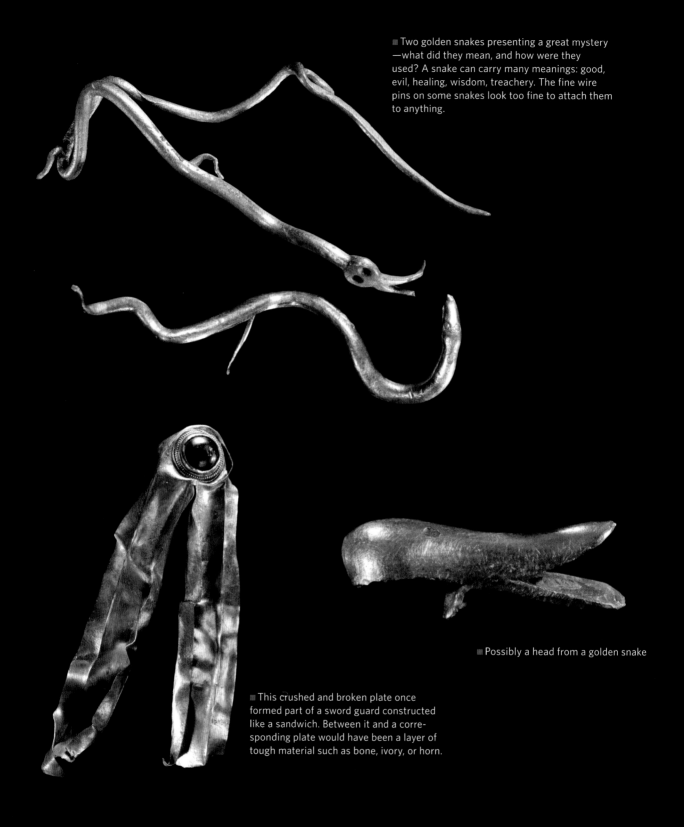

■ Two golden snakes presenting a great mystery —what did they mean, and how were they used? A snake can carry many meanings: good, evil, healing, wisdom, treachery. The fine wire pins on some snakes look too fine to attach them to anything.

■ Possibly a head from a golden snake

■ This crushed and broken plate once formed part of a sword guard constructed like a sandwich. Between it and a corresponding plate would have been a layer of tough material such as bone, ivory, or horn.

Gold and garnet setting containing a glass gem. Both glass and enamel were materials used by the Celts, not the Anglo-Saxons, and this glass gem may have come from a Welsh workshop.

This remarkable conical object is made of gold and set with garnets. It contains small panels showing two animals (see detail at right) each trying to bite off the other's only leg. Its function is unknown.

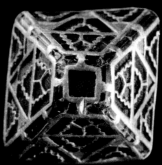

Side and top view of a sword pyramid. Its underside is hollow, with a bar across its open mouth. A strap fitted around the bar would have held the sword in its scabbard.

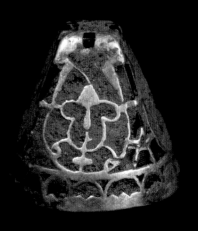

Sword pyramid decorated with two birds facing each other, their heads down and open beaks touching. At the top their tails cross.

ACKNOWLEDGMENTS

OF THE MANY ACKNOWLEDGMENTS OF THANKS due for the production of this book by National Geographic and myself, the first must be made to Dr. Kevin Leahy of the Portable Antiquities Scheme for his generous guidance and expertise throughout the entire editorial process; on a more personal note, I would like to thank Dr. Leahy and his wife, Dianne, for their hospitality to me during my visit to the magic kingdom of Lindsey.

Thanks are also due the curators and staff of the Birmingham Museums and Art Gallery and Potteries Museum and Art Gallery, Stoke-on-Trent, for their enthusiasm and advice, and particularly to Simon Cane, David Symons, and Deb Klemperer. Roger Bland of the British Museum provided guidance at the outset of this project. Special thanks and appreciation must also be made to Terry Herbert, who discovered the Staffordshire Hoard in 2009, and to Fred Johnson, owner of the land on which the hoard was found.

A number of scholars gave generously of their time, and I would like to thank Ian Blair, Nicholas Brooks, James Campbell, Guy Halsall, Karen Jolly, Simon Keynes, Elizabeth Okasha, Patrick Périn, Mattias Jakobsson, and Della Hooke. Chris and Carol Lloyd gave me a warm welcome in Repton, Derbyshire, and an informative tour of the atmospheric Anglo-Saxon crypt of St. Wystan's.

National Geographic Society staff and contractors deserving of special thanks include Val Mattingly, Michelle Harris, Imad Aoun, Elizabeth Snodgrass, Sanaa Akkach, Jane Menyawi, Symmie Newhouse, Judith Klein, Carl Mehler, and Agnes Tabah. It was a great privilege to be linked to Rob Clark, whose magnificent photographic work is showcased in this book. Particular thanks are owed to Lisa Thomas for her management of this sprawling project with such professionalism and tact. I would also like to thank Oliver Payne, my editor at *National Geographic* magazine, for sending me on my way to Middle Earth.

Closer to home I would like to thank, as always, George Butler and my agent, Anthony Sheil, and Frank Blair for his fearlessly close readings of the text.

ILLUSTRATION CREDITS

Sources and Suggested Reading

Entries are grouped thematically and by order of appearance. Page numbers in parentheses refer to the page on which a quote being cited appears.

Preface

Kevin Leahy et al., "The Staffordshire (Ogley Hay) hoard: Recovery of a treasure." *Antiquity* 85 (2011): 202-220.

The Coming of the Saxons

Gildas, *On the Ruin of Britain,* trans. J. A. Giles. Serenity Publishers, 2009.

Nennius, *The History of the Britons,* Attributed to Nennius, trans. Richard Rowley. Llanerch Press, 2005.

Julius Caesar, *Gallic Wars,* Books 4 and 5 in Caesar's *Commentaries on the Gallic and Civil Wars,* trans. W. A. McDevitte and W. S. Bohn. BiblioBazaar, 2009. (p. 22)

Tacitus, *The Agricola and Germanic* of Tacitus: With a Revised Text, English Notes and Maps (Nabu Press, 2010) (p. 24)

Bede, *The Ecclesiastical History of the English People,* ed. Judith McClure and Roger Collins. Oxford University Press, 2008.

These more obscure primary sources are also quoted in the text.

Procopius, *De Bello Gothico,* 8.20.6-10 in *History of the Wars.* Loeb Classical Library, 1928. (p. 49)

Cassius Dio, *Roman History,* Books 39, 40, 60, 62. Loeb Classical Library, 1914, 1925.

Strabo, *The Geography of Strabo,* Book IV. 5.2c. Loeb Classical Library, 1923.

Ammianus Marcellinus, *Res Gestae,* Book 26.4. Loeb Classical Library, 1950.

The Confession of Saint Patrick and Letter to Coroticus, trans. John Skinner. Image, 1998.

Constantine of Lyons, "The Life of Saint Germanus of Auxerre," in Thomas Noble and Thomas Head, eds., *Soldiers of Christ: Saints and Saints' Lives from Late Antiquity and the Early Middle Ages.* Pennsylvania State University, 1994.

Zosimus, *New History,* VI.5.2-3. Green and Chaplin, 1814.

Suetonius, "The Deified Julius," in *Lives of the Caesars.* Loeb Classical Texts, 1998.

"Gallic Chronicle," in Steven Muhlberger, *The Fifth-Century Chroniclers: Prosper, Hydatius, and the Gallic Chronicler of 452.* Francis Cairns Publications Ltd, 1990.

Dominic Powlesland, "Early Anglo Saxon Settlements, Structures, Farms and Layout," in John Hines, ed., *The Anglo-Saxons From the Migration Period to the Eighth Century.* Boydell, 1997, 101-124.

Barry Cunliffe, *Iron Age Britain.* English Heritage, 2004.

Richard Hobbs and Ralph Jackson, *Roman Britain.* British Museum Press, 2010.

Guy de la Bédoyère, *Roman Towns in Britain.* English Heritage, 1992.

Paul Bidwell, *Roman Forts in Britain.* The History Press, 2007.

Robin Birley, *Vindolanda: A Roman Frontier Fort on Hadrian's Wall.* Amberley, 2009.

Kenneth Dark, *Britain and the End of the Roman Empire.* Tempus, 2002.

A. S. Esmonde Cleary, *The Ending of Roman Britain.* Routledge, 2000.

Thomas Green, *Concepts of Arthur.* Tempus, 2007.

Michael Wood, *In Search of the Dark Ages,* rev. ed. Checkmark Books, 2001.

Nick Higham, "From Sub-Roman Britain to Anglo-Saxon England: Debating the Insular Dark Ages," *History Compass* 2 (2004): 1-29.

Christine Haughton and Dominic Powlesland, *West Heslerton: The Anglian Cemetery*. Landscape Research Centre Ltd, 1999.

The Anglo-Saxons From the Migration Period to the Eighth Century: An Ethnographic Perspective, ed. John Hines. Boydell Press, 2003.

James Campbell, Eric John, and Patrick Wormald, *The Anglo-Saxons*. Penguin History, 1991.

Dorothy Whitelock, *The Beginnings of English Society*, rev. ed. Penguin, 1987.

Samantha Glasswell, *The Earliest English*. Tempus, 2002.

Sally Crawford, *Anglo-Saxon Britain: 400-790*. Shire Living Histories, 2011.

Heinrich Härke, " 'Warrior Graves'? The Background of the Anglo-Saxon Weapon Burial Rite." *Past & Present*, no. 126 (February 1990): 22-43.

Kevin Leahy, *The Anglo-Saxon Kingdom of Lindsey*. Tempus, 2007. (p. 46)

D. Hooke, *The Landscape of Anglo-Saxon England*. Leicester University Press, 1998.

KILLING WEAPONS

The Anglo Saxon Chronicle, trans. and ed. Michael Swanton, Weidenfeld and Nicolson, 1997.

Sidonius Apollinaris, *The Letters of Sidonius*, Book IV. 20, trans. O. M. Dalton. Oxford Clarendon Press, 1915.

Tacitus, *Agricola and Germania*, trans. Harold Mattingly, ed. J. Rives. Penguin Classics, 2010.

Bede, *The Ecclesiastical History of the English People*, ed. Judith McClure and Roger Collins. Oxford University Press, 2008.

Flavius Vegetius Renatus, *On Roman Military Matters*, trans. John Clarke. Forgotten Books, 2008.

Beowulf, trans. Seamus Heaney. W. W. Norton, 2000. (p. 76)

The Anglo-Saxon World: An Anthology, trans. Kevin Crossley-Holland. Oxford University Press , 2009.

Norse poem quoted from Dorothy Whitelock, *The Beginnings of English Society*. Penguin, 1956. (p. 73)

Dorothy Whitelock, *English Historical Documents c. 500-1042*. Oxford University Press, 1968.

Samantha Glasswell, *The Earliest English*. Tempus, 2002.

Sally Crawford, *Anglo-Saxon Britain: 400-790*. Shire Living Histories, 2011.

Richard Abels, *Lordship and Military Obligation in Anglo-Saxon England*. University of California Press, 1988.

Rosamond Faith, *The English Peasantry and the Growth of Lordship*. Leicester University Press, 1999.

Leslie Alcock, *Economy, Society and Warfare Among the Britons and Saxons 400-800 A.D.* University of Wales Press, 1987.

Guy Halsall, *Warfare and Society in the Barbarian West, 450-900*. Routledge, 2003.

S. C. Hawkes, ed., *Weapons and Warfare in Anglo-Saxon England*. Oxford University Committee for Archaeology, 1989. See especially S. J. Wenham, "Anatomical Interpretations of Anglo-Saxon Weapon Injuries," (pp. 66-67), and Hilda Ellis Davidson, "The Training of Warriors," *Weapons and Warfare in Anglo-Saxon England*.

Hilda Davidson, *The Sword in Anglo-Saxon England: Its Archaeology and Literature*. Boydell Press, 1998. (pp. 66, 72)

Kevin Leahy, *Anglo-Saxon Crafts*. Tempus, 2003.

Heinrich Härke, " 'Warrior Graves'? The Background of the Anglo-Saxon Weapon Burial Rite," *Past & Present*, no. 126 (February 1990): 22-43.

Mary Gerstein, "Germanic *Warg*: The Outlaw as Werwolf" in Gerald James Larson, C. Scott Littleton, and Jaan Puhvel eds., *Myth in Indo-European Antiquity*. University of California Press, 1974, 131-56.

Angela Care Evans, *The Sutton Hoo Ship Burial*, rev. ed. British Museum Press, 2008.

Stephen Pollington, *Anglo-Saxon Burial Mounds*. Anglo-Saxon Books, 2008.

Sally Crawford, "Votive deposition, religion and the Anglo-Saxon furnished burial ritual." *World Archaeology*, 36 (1) (2004): 87-102.

R. Merrifield, *The Archaeology of Ritual and Magic*. New Amsterdam Books, 1988.

The Battle for the Soul

Julius Caesar, *Gallic Wars*, Books 4 and 5 in Caesar's *Commentaries on the Gallic and Civil Wars*, trans. W. A. McDevitte and W. S. Bohn. BiblioBazaar, 2009.

Pliny the Elder, *Natural History*, Book XVI.95. Loeb Classical Library, 1960.

Lucan, *The Civil War (Pharsalia)*. Harvard University Press, 1928, reprinted 1997, Loeb Classical Library. (p. 94)

Cosette Faust and Stith Thompson "The Ruin" in *Old English Poems*. Scott, Foresman and Company, 1918. (p. 100)

Lactantius, *De Mortibus Persecutorum (On the Deaths of the Persecutors)*, 44.5, trans. J. Creed. Oxford University Press, 1985.

Tacitus, *Agricola and Germania*, trans. Harold Mattingly. Penguin Classics, 2010.

Bede, *The Ecclesiastical History of the English People*, ed. Judith McClure and Roger Collins. Oxford World Classics, 2008. (p. 102)

The Norse Myths, trans. Kevin Crossley-Holland. Pantheon, 1981.

The Earliest English Poems, trans. Michael Alexander. Penguin, 1991.

Anglo-Saxon Spirituality: Selected Writings, trans. Robert Boenig. Paulist Press, 2001.

Barry Cunliffe, *The Ancient Celts*. Penguin Books, 1997.

Peter Berresford Ellis, *A Brief History of the Druids*. Running Press, 2002.

Ronald Hutton, *The Pagan Religions of the Ancient British Isles: Their Nature and Legacy*. Wiley-Blackwell, 1993.

H. R. Ellis Davidson, *Gods and Myths of Northern Europe*. Penguin Books, 1965.

David Wilson, *Anglo-Saxon Paganism*. Routledge, 1992.

Jody Joy, *Lindow Man*. British Museum Press, 2009.

Albany F. Major, "Ship Burials in Scandinavian Lands and the Beliefs That Underlie Them," *Folk-Lore; Transactions of the Folk-Lore Society* xxxv, no. 2 (June 1924): 113-150.

H. Mayr-Harting, *The Coming of Christianity to Anglo-Saxon England*, 3rd ed. Pennsylvania State University Press, 1991.

Paul Cavill, *Anglo-Saxon Christianity*. Fount, 1999.

John Blair, *The Church in Anglo-Saxon Society*. Oxford University Press, 2006.

Sarah Foot, *Monastic Life in Anglo-Saxon England, c. 600-900*. Cambridge University Press, 2006.

Benedicta Ward, *A True Easter: The Synod of Whitby 664 AD*. Cistercian Publications, 2008.

Gale R. Owen, *Rites and Religions of the Anglo-Saxons*. Barnes and Noble, 1997.

Bill Griffiths, *Aspects of Anglo-Saxon Magic*, rev. ed. Anglo-Saxon Books, 2006. (p. 105)

Stephen Pollington, *Leechcraft: Early English Charms, Plantlore and Healing*. Anglo-Saxon Books, 2008.

Karen Louise Jolly, *Popular Religion in Late Saxon England: Elf Charms in Context*. University of North Carolina Press, 1996. (p. 87)

The Language of Middle Earth

Julius Caesar, *Gallic Wars*, Book 6 in Caesar's *Commentaries on the Gallic and Civil Wars*, trans. W. A. McDevitte and W. S. Bohn. BiblioBazaar, 2009.

Tacitus, *Agricola and Germania*, trans. Harold Mattingly. Penguin Classics, 2010.

The Norse Myths, Kevin Crossley-Holland, trans. Pantheon, 1981.

Beowulf, trans. Seamus Heaney. W. W. Norton, 2000.

The Anglo-Saxon World: An Anthology, trans. Kevin Crossley-Holland. Oxford University Press, 2009. (pp. 126, 129, 139, 144)

Cosette Faust and Stith Thompson, "Caedmon's Hymn" in *Old English Poems.* Scott, Foresman and Company, 1918. (p. 131)

Cosette Faust and Stith Thompson "Wife's Lament" in *Old English Poems.* Scott, Foresman and Company, 1918. (p. 139)

The Earliest English Poems, trans. Michael Alexander. Penguin, 1992.

The Cambridge Introduction to Anglo-Saxon Literature, ed. Hugh Magennis. Cambridge University Press, 2011.

Bede, *The Ecclesiastical History of the English People,* ed. Judith McClure and Roger Collins. Oxford University Press, 2008.

Alfred the Great: Asser's Life of King Alfred and Other Contemporary Sources, trans. Simon Keynes. Penguin Classics, 1984.

Douglas Dales, *Mind Intent on God: The Prayers and Spiritual Writings of Alcuin.* Canterbury Press, 2004.

Christopher A. Jones, *Aelfric's Letter to the Monks of Eynsham.* Cambridge University Press, 2007.

Felix's Life of Saint Guthlac, trans. Bertram Colgrave. Cambridge University Press, 1985.

Two Lives of Saint Cuthbert, trans. Bertram Colgrave. Cambridge University Press, 1985.

Bill Griffiths, *Aspects of Anglo-Saxon Magic,* rev. ed. Anglo-Saxon Books, 2006.

Brandon Hawk, "Staffordshire Hoard Item Number 550, A Ward Against Evil," *Notes and Queries* 58 (June 2011): 1-3.

Michael Hunter, "Germanic and Roman antiquity and the sense of the past in Anglo-Saxon England," *Anglo-Saxon England* 3 (1974): 29-50.

Bruce Mitchell, *An Invitation to Old English and Anglo-Saxon England.* Wiley-Blackwell, 1994.

Michelle P. Brown, *The Lindisfarne Gospels: Society, Spirituality, and the Scribe.* University of Toronto Press, 2003.

Benjamin Merkle, *The White Horse King: The Life of Alfred the Great.* Thomas Nelson, 2009.

Clinton Albertson, *Anglo-Saxon Saints and Heroes.* Fordham University Press, 1967.

GOLD IN THE GROUND

The Anglo-Saxon World: An Anthology, trans. Kevin Crossley-Holland. Oxford University Press, 2009, 143. (p. 148)

Beowulf, trans. Seamus Heaney. W. W. Norton, 2000, vv. 3043ff. (p. 183)

Bede, *The Ecclesiastical History of the English People,* Book III, edited by Judith McClure and Roger Collins. Oxford University Press, 2008. (pp. 152, 169-170)

The Anglo-Saxon Chronicle, trans. and ed. Michael Swanton, Weidenfeld and Nicolson, 1997.

Jenny Rowland, *Early Welsh Saga Poetry: A Study and Edition of the Englynion.* D. S. Brewer, 1990. (pp. 170, 174)

Peter Ellis, *Wall Roman Site.* English Heritage, 2004.

Place-names, Language and the Anglo-Saxon Landscape, ed. Nicholas Higham and Martin Ryan. Boydell Press, 2011.

Barbara Yorke, *Kings and Kingdoms of Early Anglo-Saxon England.* Routledge, 1997.

Michelle Brown and Carol Farr, *Mercia.* Continuum, 2005.

Ian Walker, *Mercia and the Making of England.* Tempus, 2000.

A History of Staffordshire, ed. M. W. Greenslade and D. G. Stuart, 2nd ed. Phillimore and Company, 1998.

Papers from The Staffordshire Hoard Symposium, posted by the Portable Antiquities Scheme, www.finds.org.uk/staffshoardsymposium.

Charlotte Behr, "The Symbolic Nature of Gold in Magical and Religious Contexts."

Nicholas Brooks, "The Staffordshire Hoard and the Mercian Royal Court."

Benjamin Gearey, "The Potential of Environmental Archaeology and Geoarchaeology at the Site of the Staffordshire Hoard."

Della Hooke, "The Landscape of the Staffordshire Hoard."

Mattias Jacobsson, "Some Place-Names in the Immediate Area of the Staffordshire Hoard."

Simon Keynes, "The Staffordshire Hoard and Mercian Power."

Kevin Leahy, "The Contents of the Hoard."

Dr. Karen Høiland Nielsen, "Style II and all that: the potential of the hoard for statistical study of chronology and geographical distributions."

Kevin Leahy, *Anglo-Saxon Crafts.* Tempus, 2003.

G. Speake, *Anglo-Saxon Animal Art and its Germanic Background.* Oxford University Press, 1980.

Patrick Périn, Thomas Calligaro et al., "Provenancing Merovingian garnets by PIXE and µ-Raman Spectrometry," in Joachim Hennings, ed., *Post-Roman Trade and Settlement in Europe and Byzantium: The Heirs of the Roman West.* Walter de Gruyter, 2007, 69-75.

Mircea Eliade, *The Forge and the Crucible: The Origins and Structures of Alchemy.* University of Chicago Press, 1979.

K. R. Crocker, "The Lame Smith: Parallel Features in the Myths of the Greek Hephaestus and the Teutonic Wayland," *Archaeological News* VI (1977): 67-71.

Richard Abels, *Alfred the Great: War, Culture and Kingship in Anglo-Saxon England.* Longman, 1998.

Ryan Lavelle, *Fortifications in Wessex c. 800-1066.* Osprey Publishing, 2003.

Andrew Reynolds, *Later Anglo-Saxon England: Life & Landscape.* Tempus, 2002.

Alan Vince, *Saxon London: An Archaeological Investigation.* Batsford Ltd, 1990.

Robert Ferguson, *The Vikings: A History.* Penguin, 2010.

Julian Richards, *Viking Age England,* 2nd ed. Tempus, 2004.

Robert Lacey and Danny Danziger, *The Year 1000: What Life Was Like at the Turn of the First Millennium, An Englishman's World.* Back Bay Books, 2000.

David Howarth, *1066: The Year of the Conquest.* Penguin, 1981.

The Last Battle

Beowulf, trans. Seamus Heaney. W. W. Norton, 2000. (p. 208)

The Anglo-Saxon Chronicle, trans. and ed. Michael Swanton. Weidenfeld and Nicolson, 1997.

Raymond Chambers, *Widsith: A Study in Old English Heroic Legend.* University of Toronto Libraries, 2011.

The Anglo-Saxon World: An Anthology, trans. Kevin Crossley-Holland. Oxford University Press, 2009.

Michael Wood, *In Search of the Dark Ages,* rev. ed. Checkmark Books, 2001.

Michael Hunter, "Germanic and Roman antiquity and the sense of the past in Anglo-Saxon England," *Anglo-Saxon England* 3 (1974): 29-50.

Sarah Foot, "The Making of *Angelcynn*: English Identity Before the Norman Conquest," *Transactions of the Royal Historical Society* 6, 6th series (1996): pp. 25–49.

INDEX

Lost Gold of the Dark Ages

Caroline Alexander

Companion book to the National Geographic Channel show. Also available on DVD at natgeotv.com/saxongold

Published by the National Geographic Society

John M. Fahey, Jr., *Chairman of the Board and Chief Executive Officer*

Timothy T. Kelly, *President*

Declan Moore, *Executive Vice President; President, Publishing*

Melina Gerosa Bellows, *Executive Vice President; Chief Creative Officer, Books, Kids, and Family*

Prepared by the Book Division

Barbara Brownell Grogan, *Vice President and Editor in Chief*

Jonathan Halling, *Design Director, Books and Children's Publishing*

Marianne R. Koszorus, *Design Director, Books*

Lisa Thomas, *Senior Editor*

Carl Mehler, *Director of Maps*

R. Gary Colbert, *Production Director*

Jennifer A. Thornton, *Managing Editor*

Meredith C. Wilcox, *Administrative Director, Illustrations*

Staff for This Book

Elizabeth Newhouse, *Text Editor*

Sanaa Akkach, *Art Director*

Jane Menyawi, *Illustrations Editor*

Kevin Leahy, Elizabeth Snodgrass, Ken Bingham, Nicola Payne, *Contributing Writers*

Judith Klein, *Production Editor*

Mike Horenstein, *Production Manager*

Marshall Kiker, *Illustrations Specialist*

Noelle Weber, *Design Assistant*

Manufacturing and Quality Management

Christopher A. Liedel, *Chief Financial Officer*

Phillip L. Schlosser, *Senior Vice President*

Chris Brown, *Technical Director*

Nicole Elliott, *Manager*

Rachel Faulise, *Manager*

Robert L. Barr, *Manager*

The National Geographic Society is one of the world's largest nonprofit scientific and educational organizations. Founded in 1888 to "increase and diffuse geographic knowledge," the Society works to inspire people to care about the planet. National Geographic reflects the world through its magazines, television programs, films, music and radio, books, DVDs, maps, exhibitions, live events, school publishing programs, interactive media and merchandise. *National Geographic* magazine, the Society's official journal, published in English and 33 local-language editions, is read by more than 40 million people each month. The National Geographic Channel reaches 370 million households in 34 languages in 168 countries. National Geographic Digital Media receives more than 15 million visitors a month. National Geographic has funded more than 9,600 scientific research, conservation and exploration projects and supports an education program promoting geography literacy. For more information, visit www.nationalgeographic.com.

For more information, please call 1-800-NGS LINE (647-5463) or write to the following address:

National Geographic Society
1145 17th Street N.W.
Washington, D.C. 20036-4688 U.S.A.

For information about special discounts for bulk purchases, please contact National Geographic Books Special Sales: ngspecsales@ngs.org

For rights or permissions inquiries, please contact National Geographic Books Subsidiary Rights: ngbookrights@ngs.org

ISBN: 978-1-4262-0814-0

Printed in the United States of America

11/QGT-CML/1